W9-BSI-892

Staff Your
Church for
Growth

Also by Gary L. McIntosh

The Exodus Principle

Make Room for the Boom . . . or Bust: Six Church Models for Reaching Three Generations

One Size Doesn't Fit All: Bringing Out the Best in Any Size Church

Three Generations: Riding the Waves of Change in Your Church

With Robert Edmondson
It Only Hurts on Monday

With Glen S. Martin
Creating Community
Finding Them, Keeping Them
The Issachar Factor

With Samuel D. Rima Sr.
Overcoming the Dark Side of Leadership: The Paradox of Personal Dysfunction

Staff Your

BUILDING TEAM MINISTRY

Church for

IN THE 21ST CENTURY

Growth

Gary L. McIntosh

Baker Books

A Division of Baker Book House Co
Grand Rapids, Michigan 49516

Published by Baker Books
a division of Baker Book House Company
P.O. Box 6287, Grand Rapids, MI 49516-6287

Printed in the United States of America

Library of Congress Cataloging-in-Publication Data

McIntosh, Gary, 1947–
    Staff your church for growth : building team ministry in the
21st century / Gary L. McIntosh.
      p.   cm.
    Includes bibliographical references.
    ISBN 0-8010-9095-4 (pbk.)
    1. Group ministry. I. Title.
BV675.M35 2000
253—dc21   99-087579

For current information about all releases from Baker Book House, visit our web site:
                  http://www.bakerbooks.com

To Dr. Peter and Doris Wagner
for your sensitivity to the way the Holy Spirit is leading
churches to grow in the twenty-first century

7.54

99118

Contents

Special thanks to
Tammy Felix and Megan Gibson
my administrative assistants at
Talbot School of Theology, Biola University

CHAPTER ONE

No Longer the Lone Ranger

Jesus invested everything he had in a team. The Bible knows nothing of solo ministry, only team ministry.

Leonard Sweet

"I can't handle this ministry much longer," Mike Baines commented to a group of pastors at his denomination's monthly pastors' meeting.

"I'm not sure I know what you mean," replied Bill Duggan, who had just recently retired after forty-three years of pastoring.

"What I mean," Mike continued, "is that people in my church expect too much of me. I'm only one person, but they seem to think I possess all the spiritual gifts."

"People have always had high expectations of pastors," Bill agreed. "I remember that my first church demanded I visit all the members in their homes each year. It took a lot of my time but I got busy and visited everyone within six months. Once I was done, the people pretty much left me alone to minister the Word on Sunday mornings."

"You must have pastored during a much simpler time." Mike sighed. "Your church members all had similar expectations, but my people all have different expectations. I've got nearly four hundred people attending worship every Sunday morning and I'd guess they all have a different set of desires for their church and for me. There's no way I can meet all their needs."

"Why don't you focus on developing your lay leadership?" Bill suggested. "When I was pastoring back in the late '50s, quite a number of people volunteered their time to help out. I couldn't have done it either if those people hadn't given time to serve the church."

"I do have a large number of people helping out," Mike said. "In fact if it weren't for them, I'd probably have resigned two years ago. Unfortunately there are just not enough people willing to help these days. My church consists predominantly of two-income families and a good number of singles. Most of them can give only about three hours a week to church activities other than on Sunday morning. That's not much time when you think about it. My people desire to serve yet they are just too busy to donate much time to the church."

"It's a shame people aren't loyal to their church anymore. When I first began pastoring," Bill reminisced, "church members saw it as their duty to serve their church."

"I know," Mike nodded in agreement, "but people aren't as loyal anymore and loss of loyalty means fewer volunteers for church ministry. Yet I don't think the loss of loyalty is the total problem. My church has grown so large that I need full-time help rather than volunteers who are able to give only a few hours a week to ministry."

"Have you thought about hiring an assistant pastor?" Bill asked. "I pastored a church about the same size as yours and we hired a youth pastor to give me some help."

"The board is considering that right now. The question is what position should we fill? Some of the people want us to call a youth pastor, but others think we need a pastor of administration. Still others want us to add a children's director. It just all seems so complicated. I'm not even sure we're ready for another pastoral staff person."

"I'd think that having another staff person or a team to work with would be just what you need," Bill said.

"Yes, I guess it makes sense. But, to be perfectly open, I'm a little afraid of having a multiple staff. When I was in seminary I served part-time on a church staff that experienced lots of conflict. It wasn't a pretty picture. I'm not sure I understand how to build a healthy staff."

"I guess I can't advise you on that," Bill confessed. "In many ways I'm glad I'm not pastoring anymore. Church ministry has become more complex over the years."

"Yes," Mike agreed. "I feel like it's me against the world, sort of like the Lone Ranger. That's it! I feel like I'm a lone ranger pastor. Maybe that's why I'm so frustrated."

Mike and Bill's conversation is, of course, fictitious; however, similar discussions can be overheard today in numerous churches that are seeking to minister effectively in the twenty-first century. The questions and issues raised are ones I have personally encountered in Roanoke, Virginia; Jackson, Mississippi; Kalispell, Montana; Merritt Island, Florida; Mt. Vernon, Washington; and Longmont, Colorado. Countless early morning breakfasts, afternoon lunches, and late night discussions have revealed several concerns of many church leaders and pastors. They are asking questions such as:

Does our church need a multiple pastoral staff?
Are there keys to building an effective team ministry?
How do different pastoral roles fit together?
What are the functions of senior and associate staffs?

Is there a good process for adding team members?
What staff position should be added first? second? third?
What are the legitimate needs of staff members?
Is there a way to nurture a staff that builds longevity?
How do we deal with staff problems?
Is there a way to motivate a superior staff?
What is the best way to staff a church so that it grows?

Historically church leaders had little need to ask these questions. Throughout most of church history few churches were large enough to have multiple church staffs. Only since the Industrial Age of the 1800s have enough people been clustered in cities to produce churches large enough to need more than one pastor. Even then, multiple staffing did not become a known phenomenon until the 1950s, when the growing complexity of the so-called Information Age sprang on the church, increasing mobility, diversity, and technology. However, today approximately one-half of all churches in the United States have some form of multiple staff. A church may have a small staff of two pastors or a larger team of a dozen or more. As a result, an increasing number of pastors and church leaders need to know how to minister through multiple staff.

▰ Why Multiple Staff

Once upon a time a single person could effectively pastor a church. As Mike and Bill discussed, it is not as easy in today's church environment. There are several reasons why multiple staff are necessary in churches today.

No One Has All the Gifts

Depending on whom you read, there are fifteen or more spiritual gifts listed in the Bible. Some students of the Bible believe that the actual number of spiritual gifts is unlimited, so it stands to reason that no one person, no matter how gifted, has all the gifts. While most accept this truth in their head, church members may continue to hold an emotional fantasy that their pastor (or pastors) possesses all the gifts. The truth is, however, that only one person has all the gifts and that is Jesus Christ himself. Once leaders come to grips with the fact that pastors are not gifted in every area, it becomes quite obvious that additional staff are needed.

The Loss of Volunteers

One might contend that all the necessary gifts to build a church are present in the people. God has gifted each person and, to the extent each person is empowered to use his gifts, the church will grow. Unfortunately the lifestyle of most people today reduces their time for volunteer ministry. The emergence of the two-income family, the growing number of women pursuing careers, and a commuter constituency, among other lifestyle changes, have diminished the number of hours the typical church member can devote to volunteer service.

The Change of Roles from Generalist to Specialist

Gone are the days when a pastor could focus on a simple homogeneous family church and offer a ministry package of one worship service, men's and women's programs, youth and children's programs, a foreign missions group, and Sunday school. Today's heterogeneous mix, consisting of blended families, married couples, singles, and formerly married singles, as well as ethnic diversity—with everyone wanting her preference in programming, worship style, and preaching approach—demonstrates quite well the growing complexity of ministry.

The obvious increasing complexity of our world makes it nearly impossible for a single pastor to deal with all the issues and needs of the people. Just as the secular world has moved toward specialization and subspecialization, so the church must respond with specialization to effectively minister to the complex needs of people.

The Increasing Number of Larger Churches

Over the last few decades, churches have been growing larger. Approximately one-half of church constituents in the United States attend churches that have more than one pastoral staff person.[1] Smaller churches are able to use volunteers to carry out many responsibilities because of the size of the ministry. As churches grow into middle and large size, however, the size of the job is much larger. The workload increases, making it more difficult to find volunteers who have the available time to take on responsibilities in the church. Particularly in areas requiring larger oversight, it is necessary to place a full-time pastor in charge.

The Expectations and Needs of People

Lyle Schaller writes, "In today's world people place greater demands on person-centered institutions than was true only thirty years ago. This often requires a broader range of specialized ministries in response to people's needs."[2] The increasing complex social challenges and individual needs of church members have never been greater. In bygone years senior pastors rarely dealt with issues such as dysfunctional families or substance abuse. As the specialized needs of people and families have increased, so has the need for specialized associate staff members.

The Americanization of Churches

Churches can get by with limited staff when a congregation is primarily made up of one homogeneous unit. Such was the case for many years in churches formed by European immigrants coming to the United States. The strong traditions, loyalties, and family units common to such a homogeneous grouping made it possible for one pastor to lead a large group of people. A similar example can be seen today in churches made up of immigrants from Asian countries. These churches need fewer staff due to the natural family ties present in homogeneous congregations.

As churches become more westernized or Americanized, they are less homogeneous and, therefore, have more complexity in the desires, expectations, and needs of members of the congregation. This change normally results in a predictable need for more pastoral staff to provide for a well-rounded church ministry.

The Loss of Church Loyalty

Quite a number of people can still remember a time when loyalty was an active aspect of life. People purchased cars, soap, and clothing and attended churches based on a lifetime of loyalties. A person was born a Lutheran, he was baptized a Lutheran, he raised his children as Lutherans, and he was buried as a Lutheran. If he moved to another area of his state or country, he looked for a Lutheran church to join. Such loyalty has lapsed during the past half century, as people have found more freedom through mobility, have become disappointed in denominational decisions, are more aware of other churches, and have seen churches of different denominations on television. In general, loss of loyalty is present in all aspects of life. And for churches in particular, people tend to be no more loyal to their own congregation than they are to their denomination. As a result, people participate less in their church and do less volunteer service, leading to the need for more pastoral staff.

The Biblical Examples of Team Ministry

Team ministry is a common aspect of biblical Christianity, as the New Testament demonstrates. The twelve disciples and Paul's team of church planters are two well-known examples. Team ministry in churches demands more than one leader, whether it is a pastor teamed with lay leaders or with other paid pastoral staff. Team ministry is also apparent in the early church where there were multiple elders. The New Testament consistently presents leadership within the framework of multiple leaders. Paul "ordained . . . elders in every church" (Acts 14:23 KJV) and Peter addressed "the elders who are among you" (1 Peter 5:1 KJV).

◤ Staffed for Decline

On January 28, 1973, Edward L. R. Elson preached his last sermon to the congregation he had pastored for twenty-seven years. Shortly after retiring he wrote an article published in *Christianity Today* titled, "Memorable Years in a Washington Pulpit." In that article he recounted a meeting with Admiral Paul A. Bastedo, who had been one of President Franklin D. Roosevelt's naval aides. In the course of a lunch together, the admiral's first bit of advice to Pastor Elson was "Get a good staff."[3]

Such advice is appropriate for church leaders today. However, a simple observation of the majority of churches with multiple staffs reveals that many (perhaps most) are staffed for a decline or numerical plateau rather than for growth. Churches always follow, consciously or unknowingly, one of three policies in staffing. "The most common policy is to staff for numerical decline. A smaller number of churches staff to remain on a plateau in size. A relatively small proportion staff to grow in numbers."[4] C. Peter Wager confirms this assessment of the level of church staff when he writes, "Most churches are understaffed for growth. They are staffed for maintenance and survival, but not for growth. If your church is to sustain growth momentum, staffing must become a very high priority."[5]

Staff Your Church for Growth: Building Team Ministry in the 21st Century is designed to assist church leaders in staffing their churches for growth, rather than decline. After speaking to hundreds of leaders and consulting with dozens of churches since 1983, I have found that relatively few have a solid rationale for developing a multiple staff ministry. In *Staff Your Church for Growth* you will discover an approach to staffing that is both functional and biblical. The model presented in these pages has been effectively used to assist senior pastors and church leaders because it answers many of the questions raised earlier in this chapter.

If you are just beginning to develop a multiple staff, I strongly suggest you continue to read straight through to the end of the book. If you already have a large multiple staff, then read over the chapter titles in the table of contents and pick the chapter that speaks to your current needs and begin there. You can read the remaining chapters at a later time.

Most important, everyone should thoroughly read and digest chapters two through five, which present a basic rationale for staffing a church so that it grows. You can use these chapters to design your new staff, hire new staff, or evaluate your current staff alignments to determine what roles must be filled, or perhaps repositioned, to help you reach your growth goals.

At this point you may be thinking, *What about lay ministry?* Ministry by lay persons is crucial to the health and growth of any church. Ephesians 4:11–12 clearly points to the fact that everyone in the church is to be involved directly in some sort of ministry. In addition, the passages on spiritual gifts found in Romans 12 and 1 Corinthians 12 support lay ministry. However, the focus of this book is on professional staffing due to the reasons noted previously.

If Mike and Bill reviewed history, they would see immediately that extraordinary groups have shaped our world, whether it was the great geniuses who met at Los Alamos and discovered how to unleash the atom or the young men who worked in a garage and invented a personal computer. In our complex world, we need the combined talent of a group, a staff, or a team to accomplish our dreams.

No less is true, of course, in the church. While vision usually explodes from the minds of single individuals, there always seems to be a team involved to bring the vision to reality. Moses needed a team to lead the people of Israel to the Promised Land, Jesus trained a team of disciples to take the gospel to the nations, and Paul traveled with a team to plant churches.

Yet we continue to cling to the romantic idea of a Lone Ranger, single-handedly accomplishing larger-than-life feats. Think of Michelangelo's masterpiece, the ceiling of the Sistine Chapel. We see in our mind's eye a lonely Michelangelo laboring on the scaffolding above the chapel floor. But, in truth, thirteen people teamed together to paint the chapel ceiling. Michelangelo ultimately received the credit and he no doubt led the team, but it was a team effort!

When we think of great churches and Christian leadership, we often think of solitary names. Yet, if we look behind the scenes, there is in every case a supporting team of individuals. As we enter the twenty-first century, great teams will lead great churches. That's what this book is all about—staffing a church for growth! Effective churches in the next century will be ones that build great staff teams to create great efforts by freeing members to be better than anyone imagined they could be.

Staffing for Growth

For this reason I left you in Crete, that you might set in order what remains, and appoint elders in every city as I directed you.

Titus 1:5

The drama has been repeated again and again in many churches. Picture the following scenario:

Fred: "Our church has been growing for some time now. Why, I'd guess I don't know half the people who attend anymore."

Ethel: "Yes. Pastor Smith is doing an excellent job, isn't he?"

Fred: "He is, but I'm concerned he's carrying too heavy a load. It just seems like a lot of things are falling through the cracks, if you know what I mean."

Ethel: "Well, he's spending a lot of time following up on visitors and new members. Why, just last week I dropped by the church to see him and the secretary told me I'd need to make an appointment for next week. I'm pleased our pastor cares for the lost, but I guess the administration of the church program is hurting."

Fred: "So I've noticed. Perhaps we need to call a new assistant pastor to help him out. We're large enough now that our pastor needs a staff. I'm sure a new staff person would take some of the load off our pastor."

Ethel: "It sure would help. You know, a new assistant might even fill in some of the gaps we've been noticing. Our pastor doesn't seem to relate well to our youth. Maybe a youth pastor is what we need. My sister's church hired a youth pastor who attracted a lot of new people."

Fred: "Our youth program could use some new life, but I've heard that the best person to add to a church today is a children's director, or maybe a worship pastor."

Ethel: "Let's make an appointment to talk to the church board. I'm not sure what role a new assistant pastor should fill, but our pastor certainly needs some help."

Similar conversations take place weekly in churches throughout North America. When church leaders desire to add a new staff member as a way to help an overworked senior pastor, fill a missing hole in ministry, or attract new members, the question must be asked, What position should be added first, second, third? But before even that question can be answered, a more basic issue should be addressed— what is the rationale for staffing?

◤◤ New Church Development

In the complex ministry climate of the twenty-first century, a decision to hire pastoral staff without a clear rationale is not wise. But observation of churches that have recently called a new staff member has revealed that many are hard-pressed to define a clear, reasonable rationale for doing so. One model that holds promise for providing the foundational grid work for staffing a church for growth comes from church planting.

Observers of growing churches find that the best years of a church's numerical growth are often the first fifteen to twenty years of its existence. Stated another way, the fastest growing churches are new churches. While there are several reasons why newer churches grow faster than older ones, part of the reason is directly related to priorities. To understand how this applies to a new model of staffing, let's look at the early years of a new church.

When a pastor goes into a community to plant a new church, the first responsibility on his desk is to find some new people. This finding of new people is evangelism. Since the new pastor has no people to care for, no program to administer, and no worship service to lead, all his energy, prayer, and effort are directed toward finding new people. With this focus on evangelism, is it any mystery that newer churches do the best job of evangelizing people? If the church planting pastor and his core group do not win new people to Christ, the new church will not get off the ground. Thus the first priority of the new church is evangelism as illustrated below.

```
+-----------+
|  Finding  |
|  People   |
+-----------+
```

Once the new pastor begins to reach people, a second responsibility is placed on his desk. He must now try to keep as many of the new people as possible. The process of keeping new people in a church involves assimilation, bonding, and follow-up. Now the new pastor has two priorities to occupy his time, energy, and thought. He must continue to reach out and find new people while trying to keep as many people as possible. The priorities on his desk now look like the following.

Finding People	Keeping People

At this point the new ministry begins to increase in complexity. A third priority is placed on the pastor's desk. The pastor must begin to lead a celebration of the Lord with his people. This is the worship service of the church. In the normal course of the planting of a church, the public worship service starts after a significant mass of people has been gathered to ensure a celebrative worship event. This places additional responsibility on the pastor's desk, as he must now begin to coordinate a worship service and prepare and deliver a message. The priorities begin to pile up on his desk.

Finding People	Keeping People	Celebrating with People

What began as a simple task—to find new people—now has grown to include a fourth priority. The pastor must begin to train these new people. In most churches this new priority is referred to as Christian education. The new educational ministry includes the establishment of age-graded ministries, teacher training, and small groups.

Finding People	Keeping People	Celebrating with People	Educating People

As one can see, the number of responsibilities on the pastor's desk has increased significantly. Hopefully at this point some of the people have been trained to take over some of these responsibilities. But another responsibility is now added to these first four. The pastor must now begin to administer the church program. By this point in the life cycle of a new church, several ministries have been started. Perhaps a children's ministry, a youth ministry, a women's group, and a Sunday school. These all cry out for oversight and the pastor finds that he is being stretched by the demands of the five major responsibilities he finds on his desk each morning.

Finding People	Keeping People	Celebrating with People	Educating People	Overseeing People

The pastor of our fictitious new church has much to keep him busy, but there is still one more responsibility that is placed on his desk. He now must care for the people that are part of the new church. When he first began planting this church, there were no people, so there were no hospital calls to make, no counseling to do, and no weddings or funerals to conduct. Now there are many needs, and the people push their concerns, calls, and visits on him in greater numbers each week. At last, the pastor's desk bends under the weight of all the "shoulds" and "oughts" of ministry.

Finding People	Keeping People	Celebrating with People	Educating People	Overseeing People	Caring for People

The development of a new church plant does not take place in quite so straight a line as this illustration would imply. It should be obvious that as the church grows, many of these priorities are integrated simultaneously. Even so, this model is instructive as it provides an understanding of why churches begin to plateau and decline in later years, as well as giving insight into how a church may be staffed to keep it growing.

Why does a new church grow in its early years but begin to plateau and decline in its later years? While there are several intersecting factors, a major reason is the shift in priorities over the years. For example, in the early years of a new church the priority is on the left side of the continuum. In the later years the priority shifts to the right side (see below). This shift in priorities normally accelerates sometime between the fifteenth and twentieth year of a church's existence.

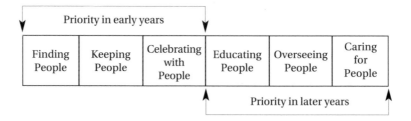

One way to envision this change is a lever on a fulcrum. In the early years of a new church the priorities are on the left, and the weight pushes the lever to the ground. As the years go by, and different priorities are added, the pressure gradually shifts until the weight gets heavier on the right and pushes that side to the ground.

Part of the reason a new church grows is the emphasis it places on finding new people, keeping them, and celebrating with them in worship. As the years go by and more people, programs, and facilities are added, the priorities move to pastoral care, church administration, and education to the point that the earlier priorities are either diminished or totally abandoned. Thus the church leaders and members move into a maintenance mode, taking care of what they have (people, programs, facilities) while abandoning the priorities that got them there (outreach, assimilation, and worship).

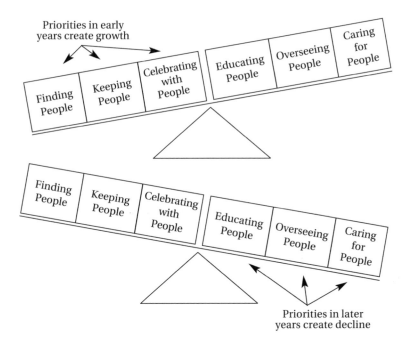

■ Insights for Staffing

This church planting model gives several insights into staffing a church for growth. *First,* it teaches that as a church grows, the responsibilities on the solo pastor's desk become complex and numerous. A single pastor will find it increasingly difficult to give adequate time or emphasis to all six priorities. A church with a solo pastor will stop growing when it reaches the limit of the pastor's ability to successfully handle all of the priorities.

Second, in the life cycle of most churches the growing number of people already in the church demands programs and care that will meet their personal needs. Pressure to provide for the people already in the church will cause a redistribution of money, time, energy, and leadership to the right side of the continuum to the neglect of the left.

Third, the tendency of most churches is to hire staff members to serve functions on the right side of the continuum. Since the people already in the church sense their own needs first, they naturally move to meet those needs by hiring staff who will minister to themselves. Ultimately, staffing the right side of the continuum leads to an ingrown church, taking care of its own but neglecting the finding and keeping of new people.

Fourth, a church that wants to grow must staff positions on the left side of the continuum. Staff members who help find new people (evangelism), keep new people (assimilation), and worship (celebration) focus on the priorities that result in continued growth.

Fifth, a senior pastor must understand his own strengths. If he is gifted in the responsibilities on the right side of the continuum, he should seek to hire an associate who has strengths on the left side. Of course, if the senior pastor has strengths on the left, he should hire an associate who has strengths on the right so that he is freed to give his time to the things he does best.

Sixth, all of the six priorities are necessary to provide a supportive environment for church growth. A church that seeks continued growth will not neglect any of these priorities.

Seventh, a growing church will place a higher emphasis on the priorities on the left than on those on the right. People in the church will adopt a servant attitude, which sees and responds to the needs of those outside the church over those already inside.

▨ Adding Staff

Think for a moment how most churches add staff. The second staff person is usually a youth pastor. Adding a youth pastor is a response in many cases to the demands of parents. Parents are rightfully concerned about their own children and desire a youth pastor who will take care of their young people. To be ruthlessly honest, hiring a youth pastor is often more pastoral care of the adults than of the youth. Obviously this is staffing on the right side of the continuum. The youth pastor is hired to care for the adults' concern for their own children. While this is not necessarily wrong, it is not a priority on the side of the continuum that creates church growth.

After a youth pastor, the third staff person hired is often a Christian education pastor or senior adult pastor. Staffing these two positions will take some responsibilities off the senior pastor's desk, but again it is staffing on the right side of the continuum rather than the left. Even when a church gets larger, and a fourth position is added, it is often an administrative position to organize the growing complexity of people, programs, and budgets. Again this is staffing on the right rather than the left.

What is the best way to staff a church so that it grows? Part of the answer is to staff a church from the left to the right side of the continuum. Yet there is more to the picture.

◤◢ Nomothetic or Idiographic

In North America churches have tended to add staff based on the popular trends of the day. A report presented by Carol Childress of Leadership Network lists the evolution of associate staff ministers as follows:

1940s Christian education

1950s Music

1960s Pastoral care

1970s Children, singles, administrators, youth, college, and career

1980s Executive pastor, activities and recreation lay ministry

1990s Media, communication, new senior adult, brokers[1]

The staff position popular in each of these periods of time was most often the one churches hired. For example, when churches added to their staffs in the 1970s, the first staff member they usually hired was a youth pastor. In some ways this was not a bad idea. Effective youth ministries and youth pastors do add much to a church, even to its growth. In a survey by *Group* magazine reported in 1989, 80 percent of 553 families across North America said the church's youth ministry was an important reason they joined their current church.[2] While hiring staff in this manner may occasionally prove successful, building a staff team based on the popular ministry roles of the time is not the best way to approach the task.

To determine which staff person to hire next, particularly for those roles that focus on specific age categories, a congregation should be aware of research in the field of human relations. While most studies on human relations have been completed in the business community, the principles of how humans work and relate together provide helpful insights for staffing a church for growth.

Over the last half century several personality tests and leadership style profiles have been designed to help individuals understand themselves better. Common wisdom suggests that the focus of individuals and organizations can be viewed as a grid where one line represents an emphasis on "task" and the other line on "relationship."

As individuals, we tend to be primarily motivated by either task or relationships. Of course, as leaders in the church we must be concerned with both. Since the local church is the extension of Christ and his ministry on the earth, we must be concerned with the growth and expansion of the church as an organization (task). At the same time, since Christ's church is a community of faith, we must be concerned with our people's personal growth and maturity (relationships).

Technically, the grid line representing the task-oriented dimension of the local church is called the "nomothetic" line. The line denoting the relational-oriented dimension is called the "idiographic" line. A nomothetic organization places heavy emphasis on the goals and achievements of the institution, whereas an idiographic organization places heavy emphasis on the needs of individuals. Likewise, a person serving in a nomothetic role seeks to fulfill the task delegated to that role, whereas a person serving in an idiographic role seeks to meet the needs of a particular group of people.

A comparison of these two dimensions might look like this:

Nomothetic Dimension	Idiographic Dimension
Task orientation	Relational orientation
Focus on achievement	Focus on maintenance
Formal structures	Informal structures
Organizational needs	Individual needs
Effectiveness desired	Efficiency desired
Initiate new ministries	Improve old ministries
Concern for the organization	Concern for the person

By using the concept of nomothetic and idiographic dimensions, a grid for staffing a church for growth can now be developed.

The roles at the top of the grid represent positions that have more of a task orientation. As examples, a worship pastor's role is to develop "worship" for all age groups and a church administrator's role is to oversee the entire church ministry that includes all age groups.

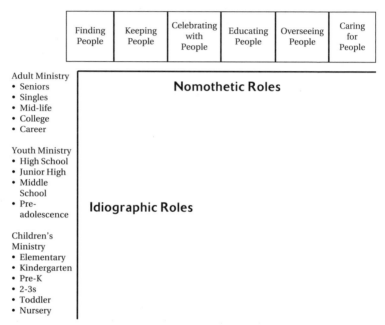

Senior Pastor

Finding People	Keeping People	Celebrating with People	Educating People	Overseeing People	Caring for People

Adult Ministry
• Seniors
• Singles
• Mid-life
• College
• Career

Nomothetic Roles

Youth Ministry
• High School
• Junior High
• Middle School
• Pre-adolescence

Idiographic Roles

Children's Ministry
• Elementary
• Kindergarten
• Pre-K
• 2-3s
• Toddler
• Nursery

    The roles represented down the left side of the grid have more of a relational orientation; i.e., they focus on meeting the needs of a particular age group. As examples, a pastor of middle-age adults is to organize a ministry for that specific age group, while a children's pastor designs ministry strictly for children.

    A balance or synthesis of the two dimensions must be present within the church. For a church to staff for growth, this balance must be maintained. However, as one might expect, since churches tend to focus on relationships, the tendency is to place too much emphasis on the idiographic dimension to the detriment of the church's nomothetic dimension. Thus it is not uncommon to find a church that has too many staff on the left side of the grid (idiographic) and too few staff at the top of the grid (nomothetic).

Hiring staff to fill the roles on the top puts the stress on the task, while hiring staff for age-related roles down the left side of the grid stresses relational needs. To see where your staff members are placed, simply fill in the names of each staff person near the role that she currently fills. By doing this, you will immediately see where the strengths and weaknesses are in the overall staffing picture.

◥ Five Core Guidelines

The grid makes it clear why the following five core guidelines are important to remember in building your staff team.

Guideline 1

The second staff person to be hired should be a person who balances the gifts and talents of the senior pastor. Church consultant Bill Easum suggests that "One of the most difficult things a pastor has to do is gather a staff that can complement her or his gifts."[3] When a church considers a second staff person, the initial step should be to analyze the senior pastor's gift mix: spiritual gifts, talents, strengths, passions, and interests. In most situations the senior pastor's gift mix will fall clearly on either the left or right side of the nomothetic continuum. When calling a second staff person, be certain the new staff member's strengths balance the senior pastor's gift mix. In the movie *Rocky* the boxer Rocky Balboa sums up the power of teamwork and synergy as he describes the relationship he and his girlfriend have: "I've got gaps, she's got gaps. Together, we've got no gaps."[4] In a similar manner, the second person added to the staff team must fill in the "gaps" of the senior pastor. Lyle Schaller asserts, "The larger the congregation, the more important it is to build a staff that complements and reinforces the priorities of the senior minister."[5]

Guideline 2

The second person to be hired should fill one of the roles on the nomothetic portion of the staffing grid. If the senior pastor's strengths fall on the left side of the continuum (he is best at outreach, assimilation, or worship), the second staff person should have gifts that fall on the right side (she is able to minister in education, administration, or care) or vice versa (see figure below). By balancing the nomothetic portion of the grid before filling a position on the idiographic side, you will be staffing for growth by further developing a major area of task ministry for the entire church.

If the senior pastor is gifted on this side of the continuum, then . . .			. . . hire the second staff person to fill one of the roles on this side.		
Finding People	Keeping People	Celebrating with People	Educating People	Overseeing People	Caring for People

Hire the second staff person to fill one of the roles on this side if . . .			. . . the senior pastor is gifted on this side of the continuum.		
Finding People	Keeping People	Celebrating with People	Educating People	Overseeing People	Caring for People

Guideline 3

The third staff person to be hired should fill one of the idiographic roles. Staff the idiographic positions with volunteers as long as possible. Then, when you eventually add a third staff person, look for someone to fill one of the idiographic ministries represented on the left side. Determine the idiographic position to be hired based on the needs of the church. Most congregations discover the need for a full-time staff person in either the youth or children's ministry, but that may not always be the case. Avoid falling into the trap of hiring the popular position at the time by doing research to see what position is honestly needed in your own situation.

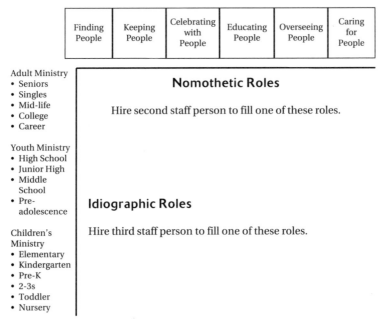

Guideline 4

The remaining staff positions should be alternated between the nomothetic roles and the idiographic roles to preserve balance in the overall ministry. Thus if a third staff member is hired to fill an idiographic position, the next staff person should be hired to fill a position on the nomothetic line. When adding staff persons to fill nomothetic roles, alternate back and forth from the left to the right sides to maintain balance and keep your church growing.

Guideline 5

The staff positions on the nomothetic grid line provide the most benefit to a church's overall growth potential. The idiographic staff positions are by design age specific and thus provide most benefit to the particular age group served. The nomothetic positions, along the top line, provide benefits to the entire church body by equipping leaders to carry out the ministry.

Do you already have a multiple staff team? If so, what positions are your current staff members filling on the staffing grid? What does their placement tell you about your future growth potential, what staff person you need to hire next time, and where you are weak?

If you are just beginning to build a staff team, what is your senior pastor's gift mix? On what side of the continuum would you place your senior pastor? What does this tell you about the next staff person to be hired for your team?

CHAPTER **THREE**

Adding Team Members

If you are planting for one year, grow rice.
If you are planting for twenty years, grow trees.
If you are planting for centuries, grow leaders.

Author Unknown

"What do you think about the board's decision to enter into a building program to add a gymnasium?" asked Lucy of her husband, Ricky, as they drove into the parking lot of their favorite restaurant.

"Not much," commented the twenty-six-year-old father of two preschool children. "I think it's more important that we hire a children's pastor to care for all the children we have on Sunday mornings. Did you notice how unorganized the toddler Sunday school class was this morning? If the church doesn't hire someone to oversee the children's ministry, I think we'll see a lot of our younger families leave."

"I agree with you," replied Lucy. "Last Sunday I spoke with Sid Williams regarding my concerns for the children's program. As a board member, I thought he'd understand. He told me the gymnasium has been a dream of one of the board members for the last decade. Apparently the board feels we need to increase our facilities before adding more staff."

"The rumor I've heard," Ricky continued talking as they walked into the restaurant, "is that the board thinks we're already overstaffed. They feel we have all the staff we need for the foreseeable future."

"All I know," added Lucy, "is that there's a lot that doesn't get done. With all the new people coming to our church, you'd think we'd have enough financial support to hire a new staff member."

Ricky and Lucy are discussing an issue that is a common debate in many churches. It can be summarized in this question: Which should come first—staff or facility? The simple way to answer that question is by looking at history. Research on churches completed in the last half century has found that the order of a church's priorities usually signals its growth or decline. For example, declining churches order their priorities in this manner: facilities, programs, and staff. On the other hand, growing churches order their priorities in this manner: staff, programs, facilities. Adequate facilities are crucial to a growing church, but in the majority of situations, it is wiser to place the priority on staff over facilities. From this perspective, it appears that the church Ricky and Lucy attend should hire the new staff person before building a new gymnasium. However, it is not always easy to come to such a conclusion.

Even if a church agrees on these priorities, other questions come to mind, such as, When do we add new staff? How many staff are enough? What will be the cost for staff? Do we hire someone from within our church or look outside? How many support staff do we need?

Answers to the following questions will help a church determine if it's time to add staff.

1. Is our church experiencing numerical growth?
2. Is our church on a plateau?
3. Are many things not getting done?
4. Do we have an assimilation problem?
5. Are there needs we should be meeting but are not?
6. Is our church becoming more complex?
7. Are there new ministry opportunities we would like to focus on but cannot?
8. Is there more to do than one pastor can handle?
9. Are we losing worshipers because our sanctuary is too small?
10. Do we desire to move the church in new directions while maintaining current ministry activities?

If a church answers yes to any of these questions, it very likely means it needs to seriously consider adding a new staff member. Even more important, a church should seriously consider staffing ratios as a primary indicator for adding staff.

▰ Staff Ratios

Perhaps the most helpful way to determine how many pastoral staff are needed comes from comparing the ratio of staff to average worship attendance. Martin Anderson, writing in one of the first books to address multiple staff ministry, advised, "If a church goes above this size [500], additional ministers must be added to the church staff on a ratio of one pastor for each 500 members."[1] His recommended staffing ratio of 1:500 was written to pastors in 1965. This ratio assumed a fairly high level of lay involvement, a homogeneous congregation, and a standardized program—assumptions that are rapidly disappearing in most churches today, except in limited geographical areas. In addition, Anderson's suggested ratio is based on church membership, which is usually an inflated number. Anderson's suggested ratio most likely would have been lower if he had used the figure for active members or worship attenders. Since churches count members in various ways, using worship attendance provides a more accurate way to develop ratios of staffing.

Herman J. Sweet offered a lower ratio in his book *The Multiple Staff in the Local Church.* "When the average urban church reaches a membership of from three hundred and fifty to four hundred," he wrote, "the pastor is already overextended."[2] He continued:

> Of course, the three hundred and fifty to four hundred stated above is an arbitrary figure. I choose it as a result of long observation, without being able to substantiate it "scientifically." Granted that some pastors can minister to six hundred as effectively as others minister to two hundred, still, in observing pastors of many rapidly growing new churches, it seems to me that the severe tests of their ability to manage their own lives, to marshal properly their resources of skill, wisdom, and experience, and to work with and through others, become evident at the three hundred and fifty to four hundred mark.[3]

Sweet's ratio of one pastor for every 350 to 400 members is more realistic. Nevertheless, few churches will experience a fruitful, growing ministry in the twenty-first century with a staffing ratio of 1:350.

Using worship attendance as a guideline, Lyle Schaller suggested a ratio of 1:100 in his seminal book *The Multiple Staff and the Larger Church.* He offered the following table as a reflection of the typical ratio of full-time paid professional staff positions in mainline Protestant congregations at the time of his writing.[4]

Professional Staff Positions

Average Attendance at Worship	Full-Time Program Staff Positions
200	1
300	2
400	3
500	4
600	5
700	6
800	7
900	7–8

C. Peter Wagner supports Schaller's ratio when he suggests, "you should have a program staff person (plus backup personnel such as secretaries) for each 100 active members."[5] Schaller's table has been used for the past twenty years as a basic guideline for staffing a church. From a financial perspective, it has not proved to be functional since it requires more money to staff a church at a ratio of 1:100 than most churches are able or willing to invest.

Based on a half century of evaluation of churches with multiple staff teams, it now appears that a realistic ratio of staff to worship attendance is 1:150. While it is difficult to financially support a ratio of 1:100, churches do appear willing and able to support one full-time professional staff person for every 150 worshipers. Indeed, since 1915 the ratio of pastors to church members has consistently hovered between 1:150 to 1:200 with an average of 1:156.[6] Using this ratio as a guideline, a more helpful table for adding staff positions follows.

Professional Staff Positions

Average Attendance at Worship	Full-Time Program Staff Positions
150	1
300	2
450	3
600	4
750	5
900	6
1050	7
1200	8

What does this ratio of 1:150 mean? *First,* it means that each effective staff person tends to build a ministry that involves 125 to 150 people. For example, a senior pastor usually is capable of serving a church of about 150 worshipers, illustrated below.

Second, it means that the addition of a second pastoral staff person does not double the productive capability of the ministry. When a second person is added to the staff, she builds a ministry that attracts between 125 and 150 persons. Yet there is always some overlap of persons who are involved with both pastors' spheres of ministry (see page 41). Due to this overlap, a second pastor potentially increases the overall productivity of the staff by approximately 80 percent beyond that of a solo pastor.

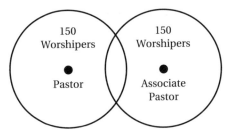

When a third pastor is added to the staff, his sphere of ministry overlaps those of the first two pastors. This means the third full-time staff member potentially increases the staff productivity another 75 percent beyond that of the original two pastors on staff. The word *potentially* is important because there is no guarantee that any new staff member will be as productive as expected. However, the potential is there.

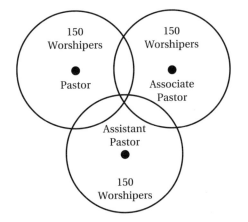

Third, the 1:150 ratio means a church desiring to grow to the next level should add a new staff person *before* reaching the projected growth level. This is a critical aspect of staffing that leaders often miss. Using a table such as the one given above, leaders typically wait until they reach the next numerical level before adding the new staff person. For example, a church may try to wait until it reaches 300 people before adding the second staff person or until it reaches 450 before adding the third staff person. By following such a process, the church usually never reaches the next level. This is not how the table should be used. The table below is more useful.

Professional Staff Positions

Full-Time Staff Position	Increases Church Size to . . .
1 pastor	150 people
1+1 pastor	300
2+1	450
3+1	600
4+1	750
5+1	900
6+1	1050
7+1	1200

As this table demonstrates, it is the addition of the next staff person that helps a church grow to the next level. The congregation averaging 150 to 175 in worship attendance should be in the process of adding a second person to the program staff if the leaders expect their congregation to grow to 300 worshipers and to be able to assimilate new persons into the life of the church.

◤ Adding Support Staff

Where is the team? Where is the team?

Can you imagine the confusion if a professional basketball team could not play because the team lost its suitcases, missed a plane, or went to the wrong arena?

It rarely happens, of course, but it could if the support staff behind the players did not do their job. The hidden organization—secretaries, janitors, sound technicians, and so on—is normally five times larger than the players listed on the roster. Without these hidden team members, the team would not exist.

Like any athletic team, a church has its backstage cast of support staff. Some common support positions include secretary, choir director, organist, administrative assistant, intern, janitor, custodian, maintenance worker, clerical worker, and bookkeeper. The number of support staff needed in a church depends on a number of factors. As a rule, more support staff are needed if:

1. The church is built around programs.
2. A large number of full-time professional staff are employed.
3. The pastoral staff are specialists.

Fewer support staff are required if:

1. The church is built around small-group ministry.
2. There is a large number of part-time staff.
3. The pastoral staff are generalists.

In most situations, the following chart for adding support staff is helpful.

Professional Staff Positions

Average Attendance at Worship	Full-Time Program Staff Positions	Support Staff
150	1	1
300	2	1.5
450	3	2
600	4	2.5
750	5	3
900	6	3.5
1050	7	4
1200	8	4.5

The number of secretarial or clerical staff working in direct support of the pastoral team is a contributing factor to the effectiveness of the pastoral staff. For example, some churches do experience numerical growth to and beyond three hundred worshipers with only a solo pastor. At first glance this would seem to contradict the charts developed earlier in this chapter. Careful observation, however, reveals that in such cases there is a highly competent secretary or two who serve above the call of duty. The work of such support staff enables the solo pastor to lead a church beyond normal numerical expectations.

The exact number of secretarial staff varies, but general rules do apply. When secretaries are in a pool, a church typically needs one secretary for every three to four pastoral staff members. However, when secretaries are assigned directly to staff members, a church often needs one secretary for every two pastoral staff. Senior pastors in multiple staff churches normally have a private secretary. This is fine, but it may cause ill feelings if the rest of the professional staff must work with a secretarial pool rather than with individually assigned secretaries. It is generally a good idea to use as many volunteer secretaries as possible, so that the budget for secretarial salaries goes further.

◾ Other Considerations

Staffing ratios provide a good model for adding professional and support staff. They provide answers to some of the questions concerning adding staff. However, three additional overlapping questions are often asked.

How Much Should a Church Budget for Staff?

Smaller churches tend to spend from 50 to 60 percent of their overall budget for staff, whereas larger churches spend about 40 to 50 percent. Lyle E. Schaller writes, "In small churches and in very large congregations, the total cost for all staff compensation rarely is below 40 percent, often is in the 50 to 60 percent range and occasionally is in the 60 to 70 percent bracket."[7] A report in *Your Church* magazine breaks down into greater detail the financial factors related to staffing a church. Researcher John C. LaRue Jr. reports the average number of ministry staff by church budget as follows.[8]

Church Budget	Full-Time Staff	Part-Time Staff
Over 1 million	4.8	1.5
500,001–1 million	3.5	1.1
300,001–500,000	2.6	0.9
200,001–300,000	1.9	0.9
150,001–200,000	1.6	0.7
100,001–150,000	1.2	0.6
50,000–100,000	0.9	0.4
Under 50,000	0.6	0.4

Additionally, he reports the breakdown on the percent of church budgets spent on ministry and support staff.[9]

Church Budget	Average Percentage of Budget Spent on Staff
Over 1 million	27%
500,001–1 million	32%
300,001–500,000	40%
200,001–300,000	47%
150,001–200,000	51%
100,001–150,000	53%
50,000–100,000	56%
Under 50,000	89%

While both of these reports provide interesting insight into how much churches spend on staffing, it should be remembered that no indication is made as to whether or not the churches were growing, plateaued, or declining. Taking into consideration that most churches are staffed for decline, it is a fair assumption that a church desiring to grow would need to spend more money and have a larger staff than represented in these averages.

Should Staff Be Added from Inside or Outside the Church?

A recent trend is to look for future staff from within the church congregation. Many churches overlook this possibility, but it should be considered a viable option. Looking beyond the obvious traditional sources for new staff may reveal the right person already in your midst.

A basic principle for adding staff says: If change is wanted, hire from without; if change is not wanted, hire from within. People who are hired from within already understand your church's unique culture and they are well respected and highly committed. Unfortunately most insiders have limited experience. If a potential staff person has been discipled within your church ministry, it is probable she will imitate the way of doing ministry that she has observed in your church. Thus if one of your purposes in adding a new staff member is to chart a new direction, the insider is least likely to do so. In such situations the best choice is an outsider who has experienced other ways of doing ministry. If, however, the ministry for which you are adding the new staff person is running well and your main goal is to keep it running smoothly, the insider is a solid choice. The outsider will almost always attempt to change a ministry in some manner.

It should also be noted that it is very difficult to fire someone who has been hired from within the church. If there are networks of relationships, great pain is usually caused when such a staff member is terminated. A person hired from outside the congregation will eventually build strong relationships, but the insider is already enmeshed in the families and friendships of the congregation. Once having experienced the pain of discharging a beloved long-term family member from a staff position, some churches prefer to add new staff from outside the congregation.

Before hiring from inside the church, consider the pros and cons.[10] There are benefits to hiring homegrown staff:

1. They are committed to your philosophy of ministry.
2. You have observed their temperament, loyalty, ministry, and work ethic.
3. They are committed for the long term.
4. They possess an existing network of friends, neighbors, and contacts.

On the other hand, there may be problems with homegrown staff:

1. They may lack professional training.
2. They may be "without honor in their own country."
3. They may be difficult to confront and fire.
4. They may have tunnel vision.

Is One Full-Time Person Better than Two Part-Time Persons?

Part-time workers are an excellent choice if several conditions exist. *First,* when the church has needs in several areas of ministry, using several part-time persons is workable. *Second,* if the church is hesitant about adding full-time staff, using part-time staff is a good way to gradually introduce the concept of multiple staff. *Third,* if financial resources are limited, using part-time personnel is a way to staff a position for much less than the cost of a full-time individual. *Fourth,* if the position calls for a specialist, it is possible to find a part-time person who will focus on a single aspect of ministry. *Fifth,* if the senior pastor is comfortable delegating work to staff and does not desire to spend time with the staff, part-time staff will be fine. *Remember: Part-time personnel may give more for less money but they are more difficult to supervise. Sixth,* as a general rule, part-time staff function best when the overall size of the staff is smaller than seven persons. *Seventh,* if the position is temporary, it is best to use a part-time person since it is easier to discharge an individual who is not totally dependent on the job.

Full-time staff are the best choice when the following situations exist. *First,* it is obvious that the ministry needs someone who can work full-time, giving forty or more hours per week to the work. *Second,* the position calls for a generalist. Part-time staff normally focus their energies on a single aspect of ministry. When a staff position calls for a generalist, churches find that a full-time pastor is the best choice as they are trained and have the time to deal with broader aspects of ministry.

Third, the staffing need is in one or at most two areas of ministry. It is standard practice to add a full-time staff person and assign him two positions. For example, a pastor may be youth pastor and Christian education director or worship director and assimilation pastor. Assigning a pastor two positions is at best a short-term measure. After one or two years, the full-time pastor will gradually begin to devote more energy to the one ministry for which he is most passionate.

Fourth, if the senior pastor desires to spend time in one-on-one relationships and provide close supervision of the staff, full-time staff is the best choice as they will work a regular time schedule. Lyle Schaller thinks, "The best part-time staff I've worked with has been more goal-oriented than relational. Their focus is on ministry and performance, not on staff relationships."[11] Remember: *Full-time personnel take longer to find, but are easier to supervise. Fifth,* as a general rule, full-time staff function best when the overall size of the staff is larger than seven persons. *Sixth,* if the position is important to the long-term success of the church's ministry, the full-time person is best.

Adding, equipping, and supporting staff at appropriate times are crucial to the ongoing development of a growing church. The ideas and principles found in the charts presented in this chapter provide an excellent starting point. However, every church is different, and the actual decisions should be made only after concerted times of prayer, solid research, open discussion, and study of logical models.

CHAPTER FOUR

Recruiting Staff

> Hire staff to equip the laity, not to do ministry.
>
> William M. Easum

Business leaders throughout the United States are discovering that recruiting and retaining key executives are the major issues of the twenty-first century. Not surprisingly churches are struggling with the same concerns as they look for staff to lead them into the new millennium. As an example, note the following six major issues that executive pastors discussed at a recent Church Champions meeting, sponsored by Leadership Network.[1] Four of the six issues relate directly to staffing concerns.

1. Personnel issues—Hiring, firing, finding the right people for large churches, salaries, and benefits policies.
2. Lay mobilization—What are the central structures in decentralization? What is the relationship of paid to unpaid staff?
3. Staff organization and team building—Building leaders that build leaders, supervision issues, team structures, and organization.

4. Resources—Making the most with the least, especially in computers, buildings, and office space.
5. Evaluation—How do we know we are still making a difference?
6. Leadership—Development and when to add staff.

One of the toughest roles in the church today is recruiting a compatible staff who are people of character and competent in their skills. Few churches can find and keep enough skilled staff to do the work, and the challenge does not figure to get any easier in the near future.

▨ Hire Wisely

Because of the complex needs of the church, hiring the right person has never been more crucial than in the twenty-first century. "When you're in a start-up," claims Apple Computer's Steve Jobs, "the first 10 people will determine whether the company succeeds."[2] We could adapt that insight to say, "When you're in a church, the pastoral staff will determine whether the church succeeds." While the senior pastor's role as translator of the big picture and caster of the corporate vision is vital, he is only as good as his staff.

Hiring the first pastoral staff member to work with the senior pastor may well be compared with choosing your child's first baby-sitter. It is a decision that is crucial to the health, well-being, and future of your church. Many times it is a traumatic experience. The first pastoral staff member sets the tone for future hiring. Throughout the life of the church, you are going to be compensating for the first associate staff member's strengths and weaknesses. Ideally, as noted earlier, the first associate staff member should provide a balance to the senior pastor's strengths and weaknesses. However, that is a scenario much simpler to describe than to create.

51

Each additional person hired to the pastoral staff is certainly important. Author Pat MacMillan writes in *Hiring Excellence,* "Your ability to choose effective people will not only determine your ultimate success as a leader but will greatly influence the amount of energy you expend to achieve that success."[3] The overall priority should be to meet the needs of your church by assembling a team with strong character and a broad foundation of skills.

Research in the field of business suggests that the cost of a bad hire—in lost time, money, and customers—can be three to five times the employee's salary. Similar losses are likely for churches that have high turnover among their pastoral staff. That means a church stands to lose up to 200,000 dollars if it makes a bad hire on an associate pastor making 40,000 dollars a year. Business leaders know they cannot afford to make mistakes like that, and it is time churches faced this same fact. In the case of churches, the loss is not only financial but may mean ruined lives, lost momentum, and fruitlessness in fulfilling Christ's commission to "seek and save the lost."

Before moving into the specifics of hiring, a few basic principles need to be considered. *First,* understand that talented people gravitate toward satisfying staff experiences. The magnets that attract competent staff are a stimulating work culture, skillful leaders, and core values that match their own. Churches do not always pay the most money, but the intangible things can be just as important, such as flexible schedules, casual dress, educational opportunities, and sabbaticals.

Second, understand that the work environment has become as valuable to potential staff members as benefits and salaries. Persons applying for your new position will undoubtedly ask questions about your church's corporate culture. They seek working conditions that fit their lifestyles.

Third, understand that the emphasis today should not be on filling positions but on assembling the skills necessary to achieve a strategic mission. A church that fails to hire staff based on its mission, values, and vision will see the danger signs: stressed staff, high turnover, and low quality ministry.

Fourth, look for new staff all the time. Do not wait until you have an opening. Be aware of potential staff everywhere you turn. Make a short list of people you admire and would like to see added to your staff in the future. Some of those you add to your list will be ready to join your staff when there is an opening.

Fifth, remember the Rule of Three. One, it takes three years before even the best hire performs at her peak. Two, it often takes three tries to get the right person, especially for a key position. Three, churches usually invest three times more energy and time into making a financial decision than they do a hiring decision. Thus it is time to get as rigorous about recruiting associate staff as about other parts of your church ministry.

Sixth, remember that your goal as leader of the staff is not to recruit ministers but to recruit equippers who can train and develop others to minister.

Seventh, remember there are no shortcuts. It takes time to find the right people, time to train them, and time to get them acclimated to your church culture.

◤ Choose Quality

C. Peter Wagner suggests that in a growing church both the quantity and the quality of the staff is important. Chapter three discussed the quantity of staff needed to maintain a growing church, but quality of staff is also a key component. The basic qualities to look for are giftedness, loyalty, leadership, and enthusiasm. Dr. Wagner offers foundational advice concerning staff quality. *First,* recruit new staff on the basis of spiritual gifts. *Second,* recruit new staff on the basis of devotion to the senior pastor. *Third,* be sure the new staff members heartily buy into the philosophy of ministry of the church.[4]

Dr. Charles Olsen, executive pastor of Rolling Hills Covenant Church located in Southern California, searches for associate pastoral staff with the three criteria of character, competence, and compatibility.[5] According to Dr. Olsen, an effective pastoral staff member should possess a heart of godliness (character), an ability to perform successfully (competence), and a congruous profile (compatibility with the church). The first two of these are reminiscent of King David as noted in Psalm 78:70:

> He chose David his servant
> and took him from the sheep pens;
> from tending the sheep he brought him
> to be the shepherd of his people Jacob,
> of Israel his inheritance.
> And David shepherded them with integrity of heart;
> with skillful hands he led them.

David led the people with integrity of heart (character) and skillful hands (competence).

The following chart shows how quality choices in the selection of pastoral staff can be made. Clearly, if a candidate is strong in integrity (character) and skills (competence), she should be hired. Equally clear, if the candidate is weak in both areas, she should not be hired.

	Strong Integrity	Weak Integrity
Strong Skills	Hire this candidate	Do not hire this candidate
Weak Skills	Possibly hire this candidate	Do not hire this candidate

When a person has excellent skills but weak integrity, you may have a strong urge to hire him, thinking you can use his skills and develop his integrity as you go. On-the-job discipleship of this nature rarely, if ever, works out. While it is possible to develop a person's skills on the job, it is notoriously difficult to develop a person's integrity on the job. Never hire people for staff positions if they are weak in integrity. If you desire to disciple them to mature their character, do so through normal discipleship processes and hire them only after they demonstrate strong character in volunteer positions.

When a candidate falls into the fourth quadrant, having strong integrity and weak skills, hire her only if you have time to train her in the skill sets needed for the position. In most situations it is still not wise to hire such a person unless you can bring her in at an intern or assistant level and give her time to learn and grow. When your new position calls for someone to hit the road running, it is unwise to hire a person in this quadrant.

Competence and compatibility are crucial issues, but without character they do not matter. As Peter Drucker says, "By themselves, character and integrity do not accomplish anything. But their absence faults everything else."[6]

◥ Follow a Process

Peter Drucker shares this reflection about the hiring process:

> Among the effective executives I have had occasion to observe, they have been people who make decisions fast, and people who make them slowly. But without exception, they make personnel decisions slowly and they make them several times before they really commit themselves.[7]

A full 70 percent of companies have changed their hiring and selection processes this decade, and churches are discovering they must develop new processes also. What are some positive ways to strengthen the hiring process? Here are some ideas learned through trial and error and common to all successful hiring processes.

Create a Shopping List

The old way of looking for an associate staff member is no longer working—position opens; acquire resumes from a trusted seminary; fill the position. The new way of hiring is strategic—position opens; write description based on church's mission, values, and strategic vision; network with other leaders; fill position with person of character, competence, and compatibility.

First, decide what the new ministry position looks like and the knowledge a person needs to perform the job. Begin to examine the primary responsibilities of the vacated or new position and the areas that will require the most time.

Second, write a profile of the ideal person to fill this position, providing a grid for your evaluation. Ask the following questions: What specific education is needed? What vocational background is preferred? What depth of experience is mandated by the job? A well-written ministry description will establish hiring criteria, attract the appropriate candidates, help determine the pay range for the position, provide clues about how easy it might be to fill the position, and provide performance objectives. The more accurately you describe the position, the better the responses will be, and an accurate ministry description will enhance the success rate of the new staff member. The person will know what is expected and will not be out the door in another year because the position included surprise responsibilities. One caution, however, should be noted. While a ministry description and personal profile are important in establishing the basic boundaries of the position, do not hold to them too rigidly once a person has been hired. It is best to mold the ministry description somewhat to the person God brings to your church. Thus, once a person has been hired, allow him some latitude in rewriting the ministry description to fit his gifts, passion, and skills.

Third, establish a salary range and benefits package. It is the church's job to know the financial parameters for the new position. Expect and allow for negotiation based on the candidate's skills, experience, and training. A church should never ask a candidate what she needs or expects, but should suggest a salary and benefits package based on solid research.

Finally, determine to hold to your expectations no matter how desperate you feel. It's best to keep looking until you find a candidate who comes close to the profile you've written. If you lower your expectations too much, you will probably regret it later. Never compare multiple candidates against each other. That is why you have a shopping list. Measure each candidate against the list.

Network for Leads

Your chances for a successful hire are significantly greater if you are creative in your search techniques. Look for pools of potential candidates by spreading the word among professional and social contacts—you never know who may know the perfect individual for your church. Be sure to include church members, seminary and college placement offices, denominational leaders, and even professional search firms in your network. Let persons who are serving other churches in similar ministry areas know of your search as they have their own networks of individuals who may fit your position. Realize that you are not going to get a "10" every time and you may need to look at people who fall a little lower on the scale. Look for a bright, hardworking person with a proven track record who can add value to your staff and church ministry. Do not forget to look inside first. Some of the best candidates are in your own church.

Look Past the Resume

When a resume is first reviewed, there is a natural inclination inherent to all hiring processes toward the "halo effect." This phenomenon happens when a candidate possesses one or two wonderful qualities that impress the search committee members. So they rush to close the deal, forgetting all the other factors. Later, the disregarded deficiencies are exposed in the new staff member's performance. To help overcome the halo effect, use your "shopping list," which should include four to six major qualifications for the position. Evaluate each resume to see how closely the person meets your standards. Interview only candidates with the top-scoring resumes.

When you meet potential candidates, pay close attention to body language, not just the words. Look for insights on attitude, character, dreams, and other aspects that may present themselves in several different ways. It is helpful to require the completion of a job application. Make sure the information given on the application is consistent with what is in the resume.

Use Team Interviews

When hiring, you are obviously going to be predisposed to hire people you like. Gut instinct is useful but it takes you only so far. You need the insights of others to help you move past your own blind spots. Every resume has its flaws. Many present a distorted picture of the real person and rarely are a person's true strengths and weaknesses presented. Add to this the fact that a candidate is often able to fool a single interviewer, and you have the potential for a poor hire. However, seldom will a person's strengths and weaknesses get past a tag team interview.

Few church leaders give hiring the attention it deserves or involve the people it affects, even when those people must serve together on the same team. To overcome this, choose one or two other respected leaders, who share your vision and concur with the new job profile, to provide balance to the screening process. For each interview, bring in one or two current staff members to assist you. This not only increases morale and trust but also keeps you from being blindsided by surprises later on.

It is recommended that you schedule three interview sessions. In the first interview, determine if the candidate has the qualifications you need. This is the time to review the candidate's resume and the basic ministry description. This interview may be done by telephone or in person. If a personal interview is conducted, take a few minutes' break before the second interview to tour the church facilities, meet support staff, or have some light refreshments.

During the second interview, tell the candidate more about your church and what you expect; then ask questions that will give her a chance to tell you how well she will actually perform. Be sure to ask at least five key questions and to push for facts. These questions keep the focus on the position, and the answers reveal the person's substance.

1. Give me an example of a major achievement or difficult challenge that had an effect on your former church or organization.
2. Draw the organizational chart of your former church or organization and explain your role in it.
3. We need someone to (fill in the blank). Give me an example of when you have done something comparable to that.
4. Here is the job we need you to do (explain). How would you implement it?
5. What is the worst thing (or most difficult person) you had to handle, and what did you do?

Schedule a third interview session over lunch or dinner to provide an idea of how the candidate will act in a more relaxed social setting. Throughout the interviews be sure to be specific, listen carefully, and take notes.

Twenty Questions to Ask Concerning the Candidate[8]

1. Does the candidate have a vision for the church's ministry similar to that of the senior pastor and lay leaders?
2. Is the candidate's theological orientation similar to that of the senior pastor and lay leaders?
3. Does the candidate have a pattern of loyalty to the senior pastor and/or other individuals to whom he reports?
4. Does the candidate have ministry strengths that complement rather than duplicate those of the senior pastor and other key staff?
5. Does the candidate possess giftedness in the ministries that are major responsibilities in the job description?
6. Is the candidate a self-motivated self-starter?
7. Is the candidate dependable in delivering on promises and commitments?
8. Does the candidate usually follow through in completing administrative details?
9. Does the candidate have good interpersonal relationship skills?
10. Is the candidate a team player with other staff?
11. Is the candidate a person of honesty and integrity?
12. Is the candidate an effective time manager?
13. Is the candidate an effective conflict manager?
14. Does the candidate have a high energy level?
15. Does the candidate usually have a positive appearance?
16. Is the candidate sensitive to people's feelings and needs?
17. Is the candidate a good listener?
18. Is the candidate a clear communicator?
19. Is the candidate joyful and positive in conversation and manner?
20. Does the candidate possess spiritual enthusiasm and optimism?

Ask Specific Questions

Explore several areas by asking targeted questions. For example, What are your strengths and weaknesses? What were the strengths and weaknesses of previous supervisors? These two questions explore personal maturity in dealing with previous authority figures. Or, What was your greatest success in your last job? What was your greatest failure? These two questions examine the candidate's ability to accept responsibility versus placing blame. Develop open-ended questions that encourage the candidate to talk. In addition to knowing what the candidate has done (found on the resume), you want to know how he did it. Ask questions that encourage the candidate to explain himself. Ask for descriptions, details, and explanations. Questions, if appropriately worded, cut to the heart of the issues quickly.

Listen Carefully

Stop talking. It is tempting to want to explain your philosophy of ministry and there is a time and place to do so. If you want good people, though, it is more important to listen to what they say than to have them listen to you, not just in the initial interview but afterward as well. Ask a question and then be quiet and let the candidate talk. Most candidates will tell you more than they want to tell you, if you are quiet. Intuition plays a major role in hiring new staff. If you have a gut feeling about someone, chances are you acquired this feeling while listening. Also listen for the person's use of pronouns. The overuse of *I* could be a sign of independence. When a candidate speaks in *we* terms, there is an implied acceptance of the team concept, which, if used in her past, will probably be acceptable to her again.

Find out as much as you can about the candidate before you give him all the details about the ministry position. If you give him all the details first, the candidate will naturally feed those details back to you as he answers your questions. *Remember: When you hire a staff member, you are often making a multiyear decision about someone you may talk to for only a few hours. So let the candidate talk first.*

61

Take Notes

Those who are adept at interviewing have determined that we retain only about 75 percent of what we hear in an interview. Added to this reality is the chance of confusing your observations, if you interview several people. Some organizations have developed checklists to aid in the interview process. Other leaders have developed a shorthand code for their observations. The technique is not important, but your notes will be crucial as you narrow down your search.

When the interview is over, tell the candidate what the next step in your hiring process is and when she can expect to hear from you. Consider that you are dealing with people's lives. The time you take to make your decision may not seem like much time to you, but it is an eternity to her.

The secret to a good search is: Hire with your head! People make decisions on style rather than ability. They hire someone who can get the job, not do the job. Delay any decision about a candidate for at least twenty-four hours following the interview.

Look for Self-Starters

Someone has said there are two types of staff members—racehorses and mules. Racehorses are creative people who do not know what it means to say something cannot be done. Many times they will drive leaders crazy but they get up early, stay up late, and, most important, get things done! Mules are people who play by the rules and thrive in a bureaucratic environment. Whereas you have to let racehorses run, you have to stay on top of mules every minute. I do not know about you, but most leaders would rather have racehorses on their staffs than mules. Mules must be prodded but racehorses are self-starters. Look for racehorses!

There are many candidates who can fulfill a job description, but few who are motivated to go beyond expectations.

Attempt to draw out of the candidate examples of projects he has completed and the results accomplished. Dig into the process he used to finish the job, his work ethic while doing the task, and what he did when he was done. Proven producers will always produce. More than that, they have a work ethic that is contagious. In addition, most have the ability to motivate and empower others to follow their model for ministry.

Determine Passion

Many people can complete a task, but only the passionate gain "kingdom" satisfaction and renewal. A person with passion loves what she does and her passion motivates her in her ministry. If you desire your new staff person to stay for the long haul, she must serve in the area of her passion. Every organization has clock-watchers. Such persons rarely stretch beyond their comfort zone and usually are unhappy with their position and future. Seek to determine what empowers the candidate. Ask questions like: What part of your job do you most enjoy doing? What part of your job brings you the most satisfaction? If you could design the perfect job for yourself, what would it look like? This will quickly reveal her vision for work and passion for ministry.

Evaluate Followership

Sometimes a candidate has ability, education, and drive, but there is something you just cannot put your finger on that scares you. If the candidate is hired, the problem rarely surfaces during the honeymoon. But once the courtship is completed and the person settles into the ministry, you may begin to make some troubling observations. Projects are not completed but it is "somebody else's fault." Decisions that are disliked by the new hire are not addressed openly but behind the leader's back to other staff.

When hiring a new person, delve into the area of follow-ership. Seek to determine how the person will react despite disagreement with a decision. A very penetrating question to ask is: What are some of the things that you didn't like about your previous boss and why? It is also a good idea to ask the candidate, What will I likely hear when I talk to your references? The candidate's response is usually very revealing. This is where checking the candidate's references is important. If used correctly, references offer not only a snapshot of a candidate's track record but a picture of his future behavior. It pays to persistently dig deeper by asking each reference for other references and then calling them too.

Unfortunately too many churches fail to check references and find out too late that the candidate was not a good hire. A simple but effective way to check on a candidate's history is to call references when you assume they will be unavailable. If you reach voice mail or a secretary, simply say, "(Candidate's name) is a candidate for (the position) in our church. Your name has been given as a reference. Please call me back if the candidate was outstanding."[9] If the candidate is outstanding, you will get a call back. However, if no call ever comes, you have learned a great deal without even talking with the reference.

Give an Assignment

A technique that is helpful to see how a candidate actually performs is to give her an assignment. Ask her to complete a project similar to the actual work she would be doing. Hire her as an outside consultant for a few weeks or few months, and, of course, pay her for it. This gives you an indication of how she will perform if you hire her and gives her a clear picture of what you expect. It is like a no obligation test drive for both of you.

If it is not appropriate or reasonable to hire the candidate as an outside consultant, then consider a different assignment. Ask the candidate to attend your church (or youth group or men's fellowship) anonymously before the interview. Then ask for the candidate's observations. Not only does this assignment demonstrate how the candidate carries out a task, it also gives insight into how he may proceed if hired. Are the candidate's observations insightful, helpful, specific, and accurate? Does the candidate see problems or needs and suggest solutions?

Establish Longevity

The number one reason many churches fail to fulfill their mission and advance the kingdom of God in their community is the issue of leadership tenure. Depending on whom you read, the average staff member stays at a church from thirty to forty-eight months. This has generated a leadership crisis in a majority of churches. If the position you are seeking to fill is vital to the ministry, longevity will be one of the keys to implementing this position successfully. Thus try to determine the future needs and aspirations of the candidate. Is there more education on the horizon? How long will it take for the candidate to become fully adept and functional in this position? Then what?

Bond the Staff Member to the Team

How do you welcome new staff members? The hiring process does not end with making the selection. The new staff person's first day is critical. People are most motivated on the first day and much can be gained by building on their momentum by being prepared for them, having a place set up for them to work, making them comfortable, and welcoming them into the church.

Churches should adopt orientation practices that help bond new staff to the team. Here are a few suggestions. *First,* the senior pastor should meet with the new staff member the first day she is on the job, greeting her, taking her to her office, and walking around the church office to introduce her to all the office staff. *Second,* the senior pastor should take the time to tell the new staff member about the church's history and his personal experiences at the church. By doing this, the new staff person takes the first steps to becoming an insider.

Third, teach new staff members about the church's mission and values. Either the senior pastor or the next staff team member in seniority should take the time to discuss the church's mission statement and related statements of core values, and so on.

Fourth, team the new staff person with a mentor—a more experienced staff member who will take responsibility to help the new person learn the ropes. The mentor should be someone who enjoys coaching others. He should meet with the staff member on a daily basis for the first week, and then weekly thereafter to help the new staff member understand the church. *Fifth,* introduce the new staff member to all the key leaders in the church, perhaps at a formal (or informal) get-acquainted luncheon or social event. By assisting the new staff member in getting familiar with the church's people, mission, values, and ministries, you will go a long way in bonding her to the team.

▟ Six Cautions from the Streetwise

New skill development comes with numerous mistakes. While there is great wisdom in learning from our own mistakes, there is greater wisdom in learning from the mistakes of others. Wisdom acquired from others who have gone through the process of hiring staff members is valuable. Here are six cautions that some "streetwise" senior pastors have learned.

Caution 1

Choose people who will stay with you for the long haul. From this point of view, there are two types of candidates: Those who will eventually become senior pastors themselves and those who will always serve alongside someone else. You want to select staff who fall into the second category. The first type are good people. There is certainly nothing wrong with their starting their own church or moving into a senior position. And if your vision calls for church planting, and it should, then from time to time you will want to hire a church planting pastor whom you will train and send out to plant a daughter church. However, if you are looking for people to help you build a solid core ministry, it is wise to hire those in the second category. Look for people who will help you grow the church you are serving.

Caution 2

Do not hire staff who are "projects." Projects are people who have problems you think you can solve. Sometimes hiring these people is labeled "the heart replacing the head." Occasionally a church may hire someone as an act of kindness while ignoring the requirements for the position. Harold Westing refers to this aspect of staff hiring when he writes:

> Churches are known for their kindness, as they should be, but often fail to secure someone who has a great heart for ministry. In some cases, it would be better if the church gave the person a donation, rather than put him on the payroll.[10]

The main way to project what a person will do or be in your church is to review his track record. If he had bad habits in a past church, he will have bad habits in your church. If he had an attitude problem in a past ministry, he will have a bad attitude in your church. Hiring people who have problems you would like to solve is just a shortcut to trouble. Management expert Peter Drucker admonishes, "Look always at performance, not at promise."[11]

Caution 3

Hire only people who have served in at least two previous staff positions. In other words, do not hire people straight out of school. Why not? Because no one is satisfied with her first job. Yes, there are always exceptions. Yet the vast majority of people find something wrong with their first position, no matter how good it is. It is human nature not to appreciate what you have when you have nothing to compare it with. People naturally look for greener pastures and will move on to another church. There is another important reason to hire only staff who have been in at least two other positions. In the first staff position, most people assume all churches work the same way. Only in the second position does a person learn that churches are different. By the third church, new staff members are choosing your church and you are choosing them. They are much more likely to stay with you for the long haul.

Caution 4

Never hire a hotshot. Hotshots or superstars appear on the surface to get the job done. However, they are notoriously difficult to train and typically they will not work with a team. Hotshots believe in being successful at all costs and usually build for the short term rather than for the long term. One pastor told the story of hiring a superstar youth pastor who quadrupled the attendance at the youth meetings within three months and then resigned in the fourth month. It took the senior pastor over a year to pick up the pieces. It is far better to hire a staff member who builds for the long term than a superstar who will soon be gone. When hiring, look for people who get along well with others. You want staff members who can handle the collective process of team ministry.

Caution 5

Do not hire the least expensive person because you feel you cannot afford better talent. Instead, invest in someone who has the skills and abilities to help you expand your church ministry. You may be tempted to cut financial corners on payroll; however, as we have seen if the person who works for less makes mistakes that cost thousands of dollars (or hundreds of people), you did not hire a bargain—you hired a liability.

Caution 6

Do not overhire. Hire a staff member with the skills you need or a person who is one step up from what you need. Don't hire the person you are going to need in ten years, because that person is going to become discontented and leave.

Are there perfect hires? Not on earth! But using these principles will enable any leader to find the right person with integrity and passion who is ready to stretch and add skills to the team. Try using these ideas next time you hire a staff member and the hiring process will be productive.[12]

CHAPTER FIVE

Appreciating Team Roles

> The point of the game is not how well the individual
> does, but whether the team wins. That's the beautiful
> heart of the game, the blending of personalities, the
> mutual sacrifices for the group success.
>
> Bill Bradley

Dr. John Vaughan, noted church growth expert, writes about the importance of team ministry for growing a church. He states:

> Growth leadership must be a team effort under the orchestrated leadership of the pastor. In the small single-staff church (usually less than 150 members) the leadership team is like a duet (pastor and people).
>
> In the medium-size church, beginning to form its multiple staff team (usually 150–400 members), the leadership team becomes a quartet composed of pastor, staff, lay leaders (i.e., deacons and program directors), and the congregation.
>
> Once a church reaches a 700 to 1,500 membership level, the pastor as growth leader begins leading an organization that is more like an ensemble than a quartet.[1]

As a team ministry develops, the roles of the staff begin to change. As John Vaughan explains, "The senior pastor must increasingly function like the leader of a choir composed of sections and coordinated by section leaders."

◤◢ Leadership Roles

With the emphasis on teams during the last decade, it has become popular in some circles to presuppose that all members of the team serve equally. As will be noted in chapter six, the Trinity demonstrates that while team members are indeed equal, it is proper and acceptable for them to function in different roles.

One core aspect of pastoral staff teams is that effective teams have a great leader. Charles Swindoll writes that a great leader is

> essential for motivation and direction. Essential for evaluation and accomplishment. It is the one ingredient essential for the success of any organization. Take away leadership and it isn't long before confusion replaces vision. Volunteers or employees who once dedicated themselves to their tasks begin to drift without leadership. Morale erodes. Enthusiasm fades. The whole system finally grinds to a halt.[2]

It comes as no surprise that in the great majority of churches, the senior pastor fills the role of leader. This is true because the one thing that sets the senior pastoral role apart from the rest of the staff is the breadth of oversight. Breadth of oversight can be illustrated by using a series of pyramids. For example, a youth pastor has a fairly limited breadth of oversight, covering the youth and perhaps some aspects of the families who have youth in the group. The youth pastor's breadth of oversight can be illustrated as follows.

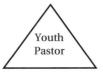

In comparison, a pastor of Christian education has much broader oversight, since that position is responsible for all age groups, from the youngest baby to the oldest saint. Thus the breadth of oversight of the Christian education pastor might look like the following.

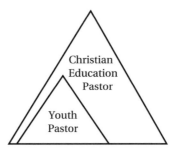

Obviously the senior pastor has broader oversight than does the Christian education pastor. This is due to the fact that he is responsible for the entire church, not just a single area of specialization. Such oversight can be pictured as follows.

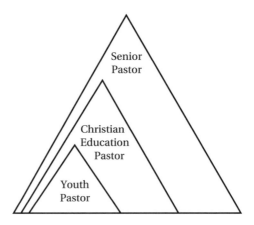

By superimposing the different breadths of oversight, one can see that the senior pastor clearly stands in a much different position than the rest of the staff, no matter how large the church grows. Executive pastors of very large churches come the closest to having the same breadth of oversight as the senior pastor. Still, even in those situations the senior pastor continues to have a slight edge in oversight, or at least the congregation tends to perceive it as so.

No matter what size staff a church has, the people tend to see the senior pastor as the person where the buck stops. This relates to the three major roles that the senior pastor assumes in most churches.

Tribal Chief

Often a main role assumed by the senior pastor is that of the tribal chief. Each church can be viewed as a tribe, which looks to a common chief for direction, decision making, and care. In smaller churches a layperson may hold this role. As churches grow larger and develop multiple staff teams, the senior pastor usually takes on this role. According to Lyle Schaller, there are twelve characteristics that define tribal chiefs.[3] Briefly, tribal chiefs:

- Speak first in meetings
- Know people by first names
- Show concern for families, spouses, children, and parents
- Know the burdens carried by individual members
- Understand the decision-making climate in the church
- Cast the vision for the church
- Influence decision making by defining problems and asking questions
- Express the values and goals to be adopted by the church

- Define the rules for planning and decision making
- Give or withhold permission for changes
- Make sure customs are followed
- Reinforce members' loyalty to the group

While it is difficult for a senior pastor of a larger church to personally fulfill all the responsibilities of the role of tribal chief, it is the senior pastor's responsibility to see that someone takes care of them.

Closely associated to the tribal chief role are the roles of umpire-in-chief and patriarch-matriarch. The umpire-in-chief's main job is to make the decision on close calls. Although it is rare, in some situations a layperson or other leader in the church may be the umpire-in-chief.

In some churches the individual or couple in the church holding the longest tenure receives special recognition and honor as the patriarch or matriarch. They may be afforded the opportunity to make the final decision in close votes and their viewpoint is taken very seriously. In many situations the patriarch or matriarch is personally responsible for a majority of the people who have joined the church throughout the years. This personal tie to many members gives them extraordinary authority. Founding pastors of churches fulfill this role since they are the members with the longest tenure. As long as they maintain excellence of character and make wise decisions, they continue to hold extraordinary power in setting the direction for the church.

Medicine Man

As the name signifies, the main job of the medicine man is to dispense healing medicine to members of the church.[4] Pastors serve this role by doing such things as:

- Preaching
- Visiting those in hospitals or convalescent homes

- Officiating at funerals
- Attending meetings of the main board
- Officiating at ceremonies such as anniversaries, weddings, baptisms
- Serving outside the church in denominational or city-wide roles
- Calling on prospective new members
- Modeling acceptable behavior to the members

Chief Executive Officer

When a group of people work together, their work must be coordinated. Thus an administrative role becomes vital to the ongoing functional health of any organization, including a church. The role of chief executive officer fulfills this administrative function for organized groups of people. In smaller churches the solo pastor is the CEO, and this continues to be true in the majority of larger churches as well. However, it should be noted that the role of CEO is quite often delegated to a gifted administrator when the church becomes larger than 800 and almost always when the church size is between 1,200 and 1,500 worshipers.[5] Briefly, the CEO is responsible to:

- Administer the organizational life of the church
- See that things get done
- Develop a system of care for the members
- Expand the church's ministry and program
- Organize a system to assimilate new people
- Monitor church systems and ministries to see that they reinforce the values, goals, and beliefs of the church
- Model behavior for the church staff
- Establish an operational model for the staff

- Conduct staff meetings
- Clarify the roles and responsibilities of staff members
- Respond to complaints from church members and staff members
- Develop a "team" atmosphere among the staff
- Affirm the work and relationships of staff members
- Delegate responsibilities to staff members
- Display a consistent and predictable leadership style

Putting the roles of tribal chief, medicine man, and chief executive officer together gives a picture of the leadership role of the senior pastor.

The Roles of Senior Pastor

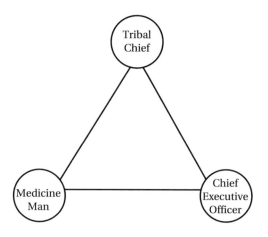

The extent to which the senior pastor exercises these roles varies from church to church, which helps explain the different dynamics experienced in smaller and larger churches. As an example, in quite a few small churches the senior pastor holds the role of medicine man and is expected to preach, visit, and officiate at church celebrations, but he may not be the tribal chief. That role usually resides in a long-term member of the church and board. In larger churches the senior pastor may release some aspects of these three roles to staff members. An executive pastor assumes much of the chief executive officer role, a pastor of care may take most of the duties of medicine man, and so forth. However, the people will continue to hold the senior pastor responsible for all three areas, even as his role changes from being a shepherd to being a rancher.

◤◥ Management Roles

As we have seen, the senior pastor fulfills a number of functions, among which are selecting competent staff, removing incompetent staff, casting the vision for the church, overseeing the staff, and managing the total ministry.

The Role of Shepherd

At the core of their work, senior pastors do not manage the church; they manage people. Their role involves equipping and delegating the work of ministry to others, including staff members. Exactly how the staff is configured (see chapter six) is determined by a number of factors. Perhaps the most relevant are the size of the church and the strengths of the pastor. The size of the church is vital in understanding how a senior pastor's role changes.

The apostle Peter appealed to elders to "be shepherds of God's flock that is under your care" (1 Peter 5:2). Certainly one of the main responsibilities of a senior pastor is to care for the flock that God has placed in his keeping. However, the shepherd role changes as the number of people (sheep) under the pastor's care increases. The following diagram of the senior pastor's shepherd role illustrates graphically what must happen managerially for a church to continue to grow.

Senior Pastor's Shepherd Role

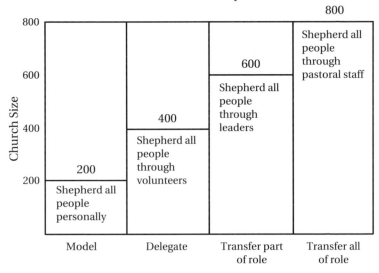

Note that as the undershepherd of Christ, the senior pastor is responsible for shepherding all the people. However, the way this is accomplished changes as the church grows. When the church is under two hundred in worship attendance, the senior pastor models care for others by personally shepherding people. When the church begins to grow beyond two hundred, the shepherding role is delegated to volunteer workers in the church. These workers may be formally organized, such as a deacon or deaconess board, or they may be informally organized. When there are between four hundred and six hundred worshipers, the shepherding role begins to be picked up by leaders in the church. The shepherding role is partially transferred to these leaders who report back to the senior pastor concerning emergencies, needs, and results. These leaders may be Sunday school teachers, small-group leaders, or a committee or board that assumes caregiving responsibilities. As the church grows beyond six hundred, it is likely that the shepherding role is completely transferred to professional pastoral staff members who are specialists in caregiving. In many cases the move toward specialization by staff members begins to take place as soon as the church hires its first staff member; thus the transferring of the shepherd role begins to take place early on. However, it usually is not completed until the church grows to around eight hundred in size, when the transferal of care shifts into high gear.

An example of how the management role shifts is seen in the following chart. While the chart compares the pastoral role to an industrial model, it is not meant to say that the church is purely a business, which it is not. Yet the model is instructive in depicting how the senior pastor's role changes as the church grows.

Church Size	Management Role of Senior Pastor
2,000+	chairman
800–1,999	president
350–799	top management
250–349	middle management
200–249	supervisor
75–199	foreman
55–74	lead man
30–54	skilled worker
1–29	worker

The Role of Rancher

One of the titles used of pastors in the Bible is that of "overseer." It is obvious that the leadership role given to senior pastors includes providing oversight to the entire church ministry. We have seen how the pastor as shepherd handles this oversight. Another way the pastor oversees the ministry is in the role of rancher. Since the word *rancher* does not appear in Scripture, it arouses defenses, especially as it connotes the idea of *driving* the sheep rather than *leading* them. It is important for our understanding of this concept to grasp the intent of the word. When used in the context of leadership or management, the word *shepherd* refers to a style of providing oversight one-on-one. The word *rancher* then refers to providing oversight through others. Here are a few of the differences:

Characteristics of a Shepherd	Characteristics of a Rancher
1. Primary caregiver	1. Gives care through others
2. Available to everyone	2. Available in emergencies
3. Driven by expectations	3. Driven by vision
4. Little delegation to others	4. Delegates much to others
5. Focuses on the present	5. Focuses on the big picture
6. Rigid role expectations	6. Flexible role expectations
7. Comfort orientation	7. Results orientation
8. Little advanced planning	8. Long-range planning
9. Concerned with present needs	9. Concerned with future needs
10. Limited leadership skills	10. Strong leadership skills

The concept of rancher is biblical and practical when considered as the role of overseer. Any pastor who has a Sunday school ministry with numerous teachers is a rancher of sorts. A senior pastor will always shepherd some people directly—usually the staff members and main board members—but will shepherd the rest of the church as a rancher—through others. Of course, as the table above illustrates, it is entirely possible—indeed necessary if the church is to grow—for the pastor's role to move over time from shepherd to rancher.

⚏ Role Strengths

Leadership focuses on where the team is going and why they are going in that direction. Management focuses on how and when the team will get there. Teams need both leadership and management. Popular author Stephen R. Covey explains:

> Leadership deals with direction—with making sure that the ladder is leaning against the right wall. Management deals with speed. To double one's speed in the wrong direction, however, is the very definition of foolishness. Leadership deals with vision—with keeping the mission in sight—and with effectiveness and results. Management deals with establishing structure and systems to get those results. It focuses on efficiency, cost-benefit analyses, logistics, methods, procedures, and policies.[6]

Leadership and management are complementary and dependent on each other for the growth of a church. Note the following diagram.

	Strong Leader	Weak Leader
Strong Manager	Growing Church	Plateaued Church
Weak Manager	Limited Growth	Declining Church

A team with a strong leader and a strong manager will grow because it has a complementary vision and the systems to support the vision. In the situation where a pastor is a strong leader but a weak manager, the tendency is for a church to experience temporary growth until the growth overwhelms the systems the church has in place to handle the growth. When a senior pastor is a weak leader but a strong manager, a church will often plateau. All systems will be in top-notch working order and running very smoothly, but the lack of visionary leadership will keep the church on a plateau in most situations. When a pastor is a weak leader and a weak manager, generally the church will begin to decline, since there is neither vision nor a well-run program to attract or hold people.

It is quite common for a senior pastor to hire a staff member to provide the strong management. However, in almost all cases, the senior pastor must maintain the role of leader, especially in larger churches, if the church is to experience any growth. Dr. Jerry Rueb, a pastor in Canada, writes:

> The larger the church, the greater the pressure on the Senior Pastor to place a higher priority on administration rather than spending time with members in a pastoral role. A widespread response to this pattern has been for churches to employ a church administrator to free the Senior Pastor for other pastoral duties.[7]

Senior pastors have many other roles, especially with their staff. Some additional roles, most of which are discussed in other parts of this book, are to select, empower, coordinate, support, encourage, shepherd, communicate with and be an example to the staff.

▗ Team Roles

The larger a staff grows, the more important it becomes that each staff member be a specialist. The more the pastoral staff functions as section leaders, each overseeing a number of people, the more important it becomes that each staff member be a specialist.

Church consultant Bill Easum mentions two major roles for the church staff: "The primary role of staff is to identify, recruit, equip and deploy laity into ministry."[8] He is correct, according to Ephesians 4:11–12, which says that the role of pastoral staff is to "prepare God's people for works of service."

He goes on to say:

> The secondary role of the staff is to be an extension of the goals of the pastor and congregation (hopefully the two goals are the same). Staff should all complement the pastor's goals as well as fill in the weaknesses of the pastor. No matter how team-oriented a staff may be, if everyone is not going in the same direction and following the same vision, trouble or stagnation will occur sooner or later. A church staff is like a symphony. Everyone has his or her unique contribution to make, but the orchestra itself is in concert with one another. Staff should be encouraged to do their ministry their own way, but their view of ministry must be in concert with everyone else on the staff, especially the pastor, if the church is to be healthy.[9]

There are, however, additional team roles that each individual staff person must fulfill as a team member. After listening to many team members, I have determined that the following five roles appear to be the key ones.

Contributor

All staff members must fill the role of contributor, i.e., being a team member who shares information. One of the things that will destroy a pastoral team is surprises. It does not matter whether the surprise is good or bad, team members do not like to be caught off guard. Team members that hide or hoard information will ultimately not be successful. A willingness to do one's homework and share the information learned is invaluable to a healthy team. Most team members see a contributor as someone they can depend on.

Collaborator

Another key role for all staff to fill is that of collaborating with other members of the team. Being a goal-oriented staff member who keeps the vision, goals, and values of the church in mind is important to be sure. It is crucial, however, that all staff members also be flexible and open to new ideas, willing to pitch in and work outside defined roles, and able to share the spotlight with other members. Other team members will see the collaborator as a "big-picture" person.

Communicator

Team members who communicate well with the rest of the team are viewed as positive people. They help facilitate involvement, settle conflicts, build consensus, draw out feedback, and establish an informal and relaxed atmosphere.

Challenger

Being willing to graciously disagree in an open manner is a valued role for any team member. Healthy teams find that they can question the goals, methods, and even the ethics of the team. In fact they are expected to do so in appropriate ways.

Team Player

One essential role that all staff members must be able to fulfill is that of working together in harmony. Marvin Judy writes concerning this role in *The Multiple Staff Ministry:*

> As a church grows in size, persons are added to the staff to fulfill functional roles. For want of a better term we may call the multiple staff an "organismic" ministry. By organismic I mean each person on the staff is not an entity unto himself,

but a part of a total organism. He cannot fulfill a total ministry alone, but is united with and dependent upon the other members of the staff.[10]

Regardless of what position a person fills on a church leadership team, it is essential that he incorporate these five roles into his job performance. When each staff person does so, the team is productive and effective, helping the church grow.

CHAPTER SIX

Teaming Together

We are in this fight together.

Philippians 1:30 LB

Meanwhile, I thought I ought to send Epaphroditus back to you. You sent him to help me in my need; well, he and I have been real brothers, working and battling side by side.

Philippians 2:25 LB

There was a time when a person in pastoral ministry had to be a jack-of-all-trades.[1] In the 1800s and on into the middle 1900s church ministry operated at a level much simpler than that of the complex and challenging ministry of the twenty-first century. The typical pastorate at the midpoint of the twentieth century was "one pastor" to "one flock" with well-defined roles and agendas for each. With the increase in the complexity and variety of needs represented in today's church, however, we now live in an age of specialization. Not surprisingly, church leaders feel the need to become specialists. Pastoral office doors display signs indicating pastors of counseling, family ministries, singles, administration, missions, sports, and evangelism.

One major change, at the heart of church leadership in the latter half of the twentieth century, was the emergence of the multiple staff. Once a pastor did administration; now there is a pastor of administration. Once a pastor did counseling; now there is a pastor of counseling. Once there was volunteer support staff; now there is professional support staff. On the surface, one might expect that this trend toward additional staff is simply related to church size. And it is true that the movement toward larger churches demands a larger number of committed workers, which has contributed to the trend to adding staff. But there are some church dynamics at work today that make multiple staffing a logical advance in growing any church—regardless of size. Church participants contribute to the need for multiple staffing by asking for more options in programming. Church attendees expect something for every member of the family. The decline of the traditional family puts more pressure on churches to fill the gap for dysfunctional families, which, of course, requires more staff. In addition, as people have moved away from denominational loyalty, churches have had to work harder to earn the commitment of a new generation. Multiple staffs are added to develop the membership and maintain the flock.

◤◣ Teaming for Ministry

Noted leaders in the Bible felt the complexities and had problems similar to those of contemporary church leaders. Nearly all of them faced the challenges of their day by developing a faithful team of gifted colleagues.

Moses operated with a multiple staff, among which were found Aaron, Hur, Joshua, the twelve spies, and the seventy elders. Leading millions of people was no easy task. Moses needed a team to accomplish what God had called him to do. Aaron assisted Moses in communicating to the people (Exod. 4:14–16). Both Hur and Aaron upheld Moses when physical exertion caused Moses to be tired and weak (Exod. 17:8–13). Jethro counseled Moses when the work of ministry nearly swallowed him up (Exod. 18:13–23).

King David also surrounded himself with a team of godly people (2 Sam. 23:8–39). During his exile, David found the following members of his staff continued to support him: Ittai, Zadok, Abiathar, Hushai, and Ziba (2 Sam. 15:19–16:4). David even submitted himself to a fellow team member who confronted him about sin (2 Sam. 12:1–13).

To rebuild the wall of Jerusalem, Nehemiah knew he must assemble a capable team to labor together. A few of his team members were Ezra (Neh. 8:1–9), Hanani and Hananiah (Neh. 1:2; 7:1–2; 10:23), Shelemiah, Zadok, Pedaiah, and Hanan (Neh. 13:13).

It is not surprising that Solomon wisely claims that wisdom comes with a "multitude of counselors" (Prov. 11:14; 15:22; 24:6 KJV) and that "two are better than one" (Eccles. 4:9–12).

The New Testament continues to provide illustrations of team ministry. The relationship between Jesus and his twelve disciples resembles a multiple staff team in many ways. He selected, mentored, instructed, evaluated, confronted, disciplined, restored, and multiplied his staff (Matt. 10:1; Mark 3:14; 6:31–32; Luke 6:12–16; 9:1).

Paul was a dominant person but he too ministered with a team. His coworkers were Barnabas, John Mark, Timothy, Luke, Titus, Erastus, Prisca and Aquila, and Silas (Acts 15:40; 19:22; Rom. 16:1–15, 21–23; Col. 4:7–14; 2 Tim. 4:10–13).

Team ministry flows from the precepts and practices of God's leaders in both the Old and New Testaments. Teams form the foundation for effective ministry in every age but especially during times of change. Moses used a team as the people relocated from Egypt to the Promised Land. Jesus used a team to found the church. Paul used a team to take the gospel to the ends of the gentile world.

Yet it is certain that each of these teams functioned differently. Every team found in the Bible functioned on a different type of model. What are the models that are commonplace in the twenty-first century?

◥ Models of Staffing

Pastoral ministry is no longer a solo, but rather a duo, a trio, a quartet, or more. Church consultant Lyle E. Schaller observes:

> An increasing number of parishes are seeking staff specialists in counseling, ministry to the elderly, education, evangelism, ministry with single adults, program for the developmentally disabled, leadership development, administration, youth ministries, worship, ministry to single parents, community outreach, or some other program area.[2]

With the trend toward multiple staffing, church leaders need to carefully consider which team configuration will keep the heart of pastoral leadership pumping at peak performance. How the staff team is configured will depend on numerous factors, among which are the goals and vision of the church, the strengths of the senior pastor, the size of the church, and the philosophy of ministry (program-based, cell-based, staff-based, lay-ministry–based, and so on). As team ministry has developed over the last half century, at least seven models or configurations have been identified. One of these may be just what you are looking for in your church. One caution: It is wise to choose a staff configuration that *fits* your team. The best coaches strive to understand their team first and then select a structure that will allow the team to function well together.

The Vertical Model

The vertical model is the most common model for staff organization found in churches in the United States. Using the staff and line organization found in typical organizational charts, its strength lies in defining clear lines of authority and staff relationships. Your supervisor is directly above you, and those under your oversight are directly beneath your line.

The Vertical Model

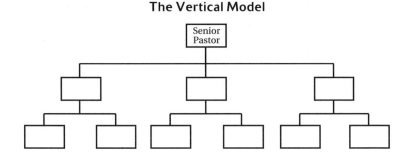

The Horizontal Model

The horizontal model is similar to the vertical model, but laid on the side it gives the added advantage of picturing a common direction much like an arrow. Pictured in this way, it shows a staff team that has a clear sense of direction along with the continuing strengths found in the vertical model.

The Horizontal Model

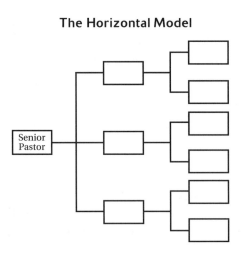

The Circular Model

The circular model places the senior pastor in the bull's eye. It gives the impression that the pastoral staff is aiming at the same target and shows relationships on each circle around the target. In this model, team relationships appear to have greater emphasis but the structure may make the senior pastor feel a little uneasy, as though everyone is shooting at him.

The Circular Model

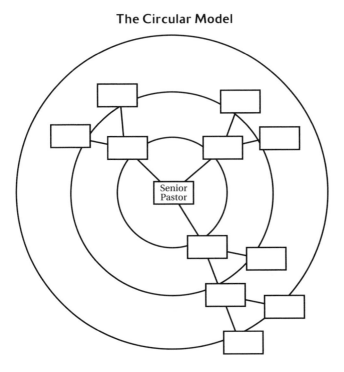

The Inverted Model

The inverted model highlights the staff team members as equippers serving a local body of Christ. Using the inverted model, pastoral staff attempt to live out the model as described in Ephesians 4:11–12, recruiting, training, and deploying volunteer members to serve Christ in the world. To illustrate this commitment, an inverted organizational chart is used since it places the people (rather than the pastoral staff) at the top of the chart. This model is an attempt to demonstrate in a picture that the people are at the front of the battle for people's souls, with the pastoral staff serving as resource personnel. Unfortunately it also gives the appearance that the weight of the entire church ministry rests on the senior pastor and staff.

The Inverted Model

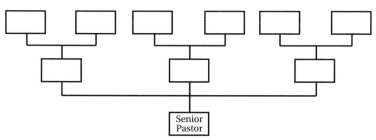

The Pod Model

The pod model gives more focus to the various pastoral teams functioning in the church. While still providing clear

The Pod Model

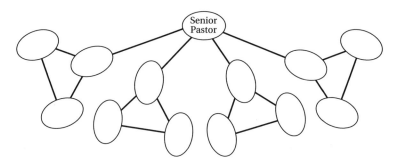

lines of authority, it helps picture the groupings of teams directly but loses some of the sense of direction provided by some of the other models.

The Flying "V" Model

The flying *V* model was named for geese that fly in a V formation. Wind tunnel tests have shown that, by cooperating with each other in this formation, geese are able to fly 72 percent farther than a lone goose and the group uses much less energy. In a similar way, people serving on a pastoral team can accomplish more by cooperating together. Part of this model includes the concept that the leadership of the pastoral staff can change from time to time as needed, just as the lead goose changes in the flying formation. The senior pastor may lead the team in designing a long-range plan, but an associate staff member may step in and lead the team in developing the church budget. Leadership of the team changes as one leader

The Flying "V" Model

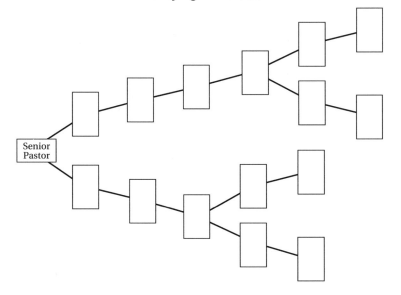

gets tired or a task is encountered where another staff member's gift mix is a better match for the job at hand.

The Collaborative Model

The newest approach to be used as a model of pastoral team ministry is the collaborative model. The essence of this new model is the freedom of all staff to bypass traditional lines of authority and collaborate with others on the pastoral team as needed to fulfill a given task. Such models are being used in business, education, and other arenas where communication across traditional lines of authority is needed to keep pace with the changes taking place. While this approach looks good on paper, it is much more difficult to pull off successfully than it first appears. Unfortunately, unless there is excellent coordination and communication among staff, this approach can become a directionless mass of activity.

The Collaborative Model

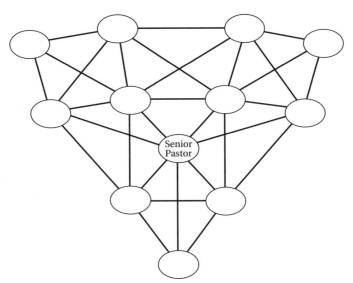

◪ The Dream Team

For the last few Olympic games, the United States has assembled the best basketball team in the world, popularly called the Dream Team. When we look at the Bible, we see several teams working together throughout the centuries. Moses and his brother in the Old Testament and Paul and Barnabas in the New Testament come immediately to mind. By teaming together they accomplished God's will for their lives and for the people they were overseeing. However, none of them could be termed a Dream Team. Moses and Aaron were not equally committed to God's vision for the people of Israel. Paul and Barnabas divided over personnel issues.

There is, however, a biblical Dream Team that often gets overlooked—the Trinity. Theologians often describe the Trinity as either an Ontological Trinity or an Economic Trinity. Both designations stress different truths of the Trinity that are helpful in developing a model for team ministry among pastoral staff.

The Ontological Trinity focuses on the fact that the three members of the Trinity are of the same being or nature. All members of the Trinity are equal. The Bible sets forth a Father who is God (Rom. 1:7), a Son who is God (Heb. 1:8), and a Holy Spirit who is God (Acts 5:3–4). No person of the Trinity is greater, holier, or wiser than the others. They are of one essence or fundamental nature. Working together in perfect unity and harmony, they accomplish one purpose in the world—the salvation of the lost (Luke 19:10). The Father, Son, and Holy Spirit do not function separately or independently, but honor, serve, and share with each other in holy love. So God moves to unite us as one in himself "that the world may believe" (John 17:20–23).

Describing the Father, Son, and Holy Spirit as an Economic Trinity makes use of the root meaning of the word *economy,* from the Greek *oikonomos,* which means to man-

The Ontological Trinity

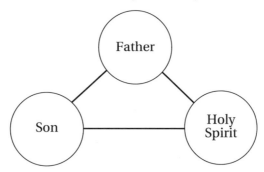

age a house. Inherent in the word is the idea of managing resources and the orderly arrangement of parts into an organization or system. While the members of the Trinity are equal in quality (ontology), they function in different roles regarding the management of their task (economy). The Bible presents a picture of organization within the Trinity, teaching that the Father plans redemption (Eph. 1:3–6), the Son works out redemption (vv. 7–12), and the Holy Spirit applies redemption (vv. 13–14).

Using the Trinity as a model, an effective pastoral team is one that lives and works together in harmony, recognizing the equality of each team member before God. Though they are equal, they serve functionally in different roles according to their gifts and calling. This is the picture of team ministry in the church.

◢◣ Keys to an Effective Team

Dr. Dan Reeves, founder of Reeves Strategic Consultation Services, has found that church staff teams remain healthy when the team members own a common vision, are focused on the task, believe in the team, trust each other, practice open communication, and view conflict positively.[3] Here are a few other insights on what makes an effective team. If you currently serve on a staff team, how many of these can you identify as positive aspects of your staff?

The Economic Trinity

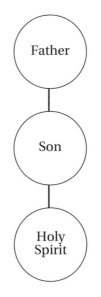

Clear Communication

When the communication of a team is superficial and irrelevant, the productivity of the team is limited. Superficial communication may occur in the form of jargon or specialized language where meanings are not clear. Members of such a team tend to avoid talking about their differences or do so indirectly through theoretical discussions.

Effective communication is purposeful and relevant. The staff speaks to each other in understandable language so that common meaning is achieved. Different ideas and points of view are expressed freely and politely. Individual feelings are expressed directly when essential.

Shared Goals

Teams do not function well when each team member has individualistic or unshared goals. When members use the team for their own ego satisfaction or the group holds rigidly to only one goal, group cohesiveness is destroyed. Teams become content with "activity" goals and always seem to be busy while accomplishing very little to advance the overall ministry.

Positive groups tend to hold parallel or commonly shared goals. Both team and individual goals are permitted and encouraged. The group focuses on "results" goals.

Collaborative Atmosphere

Teams that are aggressive, hostile, overly friendly, or demanding normally do not accomplish a great deal. Such groups tend to seek their own prestige, demand authority, and are hostile to change.

Good groups are friendly, accepting, but realistic, seeking collaboration from individuals and teams beyond themselves. They are supportive and encouraging of change and use authority properly. As one business leader noted, "As an organization, we have chosen to be collaborative rather than combative."[4]

Responsibility and Involvement

Ineffective teams discourage or deny individual responsibility and growth. The members of the team do not personally identify with the team. Achieving goals is viewed as the responsibility of the leader rather than the entire group.

Strong teams encourage individuals to take responsibility for their own growth. The members are personally identified with the team and the team's continuance and function are important to each team member. Whatever the team does, including results, is viewed as the responsibility of all.

Flexible Process

The internal process of the group is a good indicator of its health. For instance, unhealthy groups often set up standard rituals and accepted ways of doing things to the point that they are not open to experimentation. The group does not allow any expression of mood other than a polite friendliness. Time is viewed as an obstacle, and members are often heard to say, "There's not enough time."

The exact methods of operation in healthy groups are flexible and change as needs arise and the team develops. The team varies its tempo of work and allows itself time for relaxation. Members of the team feel free to express their moods, such as excitement, enthusiasm, concern, tension. Time is viewed as a tool, and members are often heard to say, "How can we make the most effective use of the time we have?"

Collegial Support

Dysfunctional teams try to keep differences out of sight, and only the leader is expected to help team members in need. Clearly defined and fixed roles are assigned to members and crossover between roles is forbidden. Members rarely have the opportunity to test out new ideas or skills but they are satisfied as long as the group seems to be making some progress.

Healthy groups expect that everyone on the team will serve as a resource person to the entire team. Differences are expected and viewed as useful. Roles are defined, but may easily move from member to member. It is expected that members will use their new skills and try new insights with the entire team. The team is satisfied only with concrete progress or results toward established goals.

Teaming within church ministry is vital, valid, and worthwhile in the twenty-first century. The days of the one-pastor-for-one-congregation are rapidly vanishing, particularly for churches that desire to grow. As Dan Reeves suggests, "The alternative is stagnancy, unnecessary frustration, and a future ministry that operates significantly below its God-given potential. Seek God's will, then do it in God's power and grace."[5]

Rueb's Models of Multiple Staffing

As a pastor, I have always worked in a multiple staff context. Whether it was a two-man team or working with up to seven other pastors in highly specialized ministries, I have observed a variety of multiple staff models being used today. Just as there is a diversity of gifts in the church, there are also a variety of models for multiple staffs.

Journeyman/Apprentice Model

Often an older experienced pastor takes a younger seminarian under his wing to help increase the younger person's skill and competence in ministry. This situation is usually found in smaller churches. While this can be a wonderful father/son–style relationship, its main disadvantage is that the pastors never relate as peers. Unless the younger man serves under a very wise and humble team leader, he will eventually want out of the relationship.

Us and Them Model

On this team the pastors relate to one another as cosurvivors. The congregation is viewed in an adversarial role and is spoken of as "them." Staff unity is not fueled by a common vision but is a function of the mutual need to survive. Because this model is not based on a firm foundation, it often ends in some kind of relational disaster.

Hired Gun Model

Staffs operating with this model usually function under a strong, hard-working senior pastor who is results-oriented. Associates are hired guns who relate to the pastoral team in rigidly encased ministries specified in strict job descriptions. Everyone on the pastoral team is accepted as long as they do what they are paid to do and the results are evident. There is little sharing of the overall agenda of the church and little personal interaction. Inadequate loyalty to the team means the "hired gun" can be easily hired away by another church.

Copastorate Model

This model occurs when two highly compatible pastors share responsibilities without a great emphasis on function or lines of authority. While the concept of two equal pastors functioning in tandem sounds noble, eventually there will be a crisis in authority.

Rancher Model

Each pastor in this model works his end of the "ranch" with little interference or input from anyone else on the staff. While there is the illusion of very little conflict, since each staff member does his own thing, there is also very little communication and coordination. The net result is unsatisfying as no one can see the overall objective or direction for the church.

Competition Model

This is perhaps the most immature of all the staffing models since it is "every man for himself." In the competitive staff, each pastor vies with each other for a place in the people's hearts. Serious rivalries and jealousies can arise and eventually someone must leave. The result is intrigue among the staff and heartbreak for the ministry.

Carbon Copy Model

In some cases, where the senior pastor is a strong leader, associate staff are chosen because they notably resemble their team leader in skills, gifts, priorities, and sometimes even appearance. Wonderful unity can be achieved, but watch out for a lack of creativity and accountability.

Relational/Complementary Model

This is by far the most ideal configuration for staff relationships. The staff enjoys diversity in gifts, talents, and functions, but the emphasis is on relationships and giftedness rather than strictly on performance or popularity. The senior pastor acts as a team coach, while the associates help set the direction and agenda. A strong feeling of unity and shared ministry develops.

From Jerry Rueb, "Models of Multiple Staffing," *The McIntosh Church Growth Network* 9, no. 5 (May 1997), 1–2.

CHAPTER **SEVEN**

Nurturing a Healthy Staff

> Don't be selfish; don't live to make a good impression
> on others. Be humble, thinking of others as better than
> yourself. Don't just think about your own affairs, but
> be interested in others, too, and in what they are doing.
>
> Philippians 2:3–4 LB

"You know it's been close to fifty-seven years since I jumped hospital in violation of orders and returned to the front," reminisced seventy-six-year-old Eugene Collins about his involvement in combat during World War II.

"I remember you talking about that before," reflected his son Brad. "Tell me more about it."

"Returning to the front was almost certain death," his elderly father continued. "I think I'm just beginning to understand why I did it. It was an act of love."

"An act of love?" Brad was confused.

"Well, the men I served with were my family. They were closer to me than any friends had been or ever would be," Eugene's voice cracked with emotion as he spoke. "They had never let me down, and I couldn't let them down. I had to be with them. I couldn't let them die and me live with the thought that I might have saved them."

"I always thought men fought for their country, their flag, and for glory," Brad said. "I've never considered that men fought for love."

"Don't get me wrong," Eugene hurried to add, "I love my country. In fact I can still vividly remember where I was when I first heard about Pearl Harbor. When Uncle Sam asked me to go overseas, I never thought about not going. It was my duty to defend my country. Yet, once I experienced combat, I fought more for my buddies than for my country. I was willing to die for my comrades, and they were willing to die for me. We had a unique love for each other that's hard to describe. After the war, we kept in touch for nearly fifty years. I'm the only one left now but I'll never forget them."

Many church staff members long for a team relationship similar to that described by Eugene Collins. How does a team develop such love for each other? Where does camaraderie find its roots? Why does a bond develop?

◤ Characteristics of a Healthy Staff

Eugene Collins's experience during World War II was not uncommon. Of necessity teams bond or disintegrate under pressures of war. The pressures on a church staff team, of course, are different but they are pressures nonetheless. These pressures can pull a team together in real commitment to each other or they can drive a team apart through disagreement and distrust. Studies of effective teams have determined that there are three major characteristics of a healthy staff.

A Great Leader

Along with the rising interest in team ministry in the last decade, a number of misunderstandings have accumulated.

One of the main misunderstandings is that teams function best without a clear leader. While this may at times appear to be the case, observation of teams throughout history has shown it rarely, perhaps never, is true. One of the paradoxes of teams is that a healthy team has a great leader. Warren Bennis and Patricia Biederman comment:

> All great groups have extraordinary leaders. It's a paradox, really, because great groups tend to be collegial and non-hierarchical, peopled by singularly competent individuals who often have an anti-authoritarian streak. Nonetheless, virtually every great group has a strong and visionary head.[1]

Reaction against having a single team leader often focuses on the fear of having a dictatorial leader. Talking about church staff teams, Marvin Anderson addresses this fear: "The senior pastor is the directing head. He is to be a leader, not a dictator. A domineering spirit in relation to the assistant or the lay staff is unworthy of a Christian and fatal to good relationship."[2]

Leadership, of course, is not necessarily dictatorial. What all leaders have in common is that others recognize the value of their contribution and choose to follow them. While staff teams do, of course, have members who take the lead from time to time in handling different leadership functions, one person is always viewed as the leader; one is always perceived as the person where the "buck stops." Dr. Clyde McDowell, former president of Denver Seminary, wrote, "Four years as an associate pastor and eighteen years as a senior pastor have convinced me that the key to healthy staff relationships is the staff leader."[3] (See more on the role of team leader in chapter 11.)

Relationally Small

It is generally accepted that the best teams are composed of twelve or fewer people, with a team of six or seven being the best. Soldiers are most willing to die for their comrades when they serve in small units. The larger the unit becomes and the less intimately they know each other, the less willing they are to make the highest sacrifice for each other. This was borne out by studies conducted during the 1940s. During World War II, the American Army Historical Service made the first systematic study of human behavior in combat. Reporting on the findings, John Keegan, a military historian, noted:

> Foremost among them was the revelation that ordinary soldiers do not think of themselves, in life and death situations, as subordinate members of whatever formal military organization it is to which authority has assigned them, but as equals in a very tiny group—perhaps no more than six or seven men.[4]

Auren Uris, a highly respected researcher and writer in the fields of human resources and management, supports the importance of small teams. He writes, "There is growing evidence that the most creative *problem-solving* or *decision-making* will occur in small, odd-numbered groups (5, 7, 9)." He advises, "If you want originality and creative contributions, . . . keep the group small. Five people is the number many researchers suggest for optimum efficiency, freedom of exchange and cooperation."[5]

Another aspect important to healthy team size is related to the unit of three. Kenneth R. Mitchell, writing in *Multiple Staff Ministries,* declares, "In any human interactional system, the basic unit, or building block, is the triangle."[6] Examples of groups of three are the Trinity: Father, Son, and Holy Spirit and a family: father, mother, and child. According to Dr. Mitchell, two-person teams are inherently unstable and seek to find a third element to make a triangle. Most couples will seek to have at least one child, and two staff pastors will search for a third staff member to round out the team. Therefore, healthy teams are often composed of groupings such as two pastors and one secretary, or one pastor and two secretaries, or three pastors. Thus it appears that the best staff team is most often made up of seven or less persons since a team of seven allows for a leader and two subsets of three individuals (triangles).

When a team grows larger than seven individuals, it becomes much more difficult to maintain the collegial spirit, intimate acquaintance, and common vision necessary to maintain team health. To keep larger teams healthy, it is wise to organize them by triangles. A good example is found in the twelve disciples of Jesus. The disciples obviously comprised a team larger than six or seven individuals. However, by closely examining the relational structure of the disciples, we discover a pattern of subset groups. In every listing of the twelve disciples (or the eleven as in Acts 1:13), the various names appear in a common pattern. While some of the disciples' names are moved around, depending on where in Scripture the list is found, three names remain constant in every listing of the disciples given: Simon is always first, Philip is always fifth, and James son of Alphaeus is always ninth. Apparently the twelve disciples were organized into three subteams. Each subteam had a leader (Simon, Philip, and James) and three team members (a triangle).

Simon Peter	Philip	James son of Alphaeus
James son of Zebedee	Bartholomew	Thaddaeus
John	Matthew	Simon the Zealot
Andrew	Thomas	Judas Iscariot

There are always exceptions, of course, but from a relational perspective, it appears that healthy teams normally comprise fewer than twelve members and are organized into groups of three as much as possible. This reflects directly on the much asked question, How many people can one person supervise? Based on the above discussion, it is probably best if no more than six people report to any single individual (a team of seven). Of course, each person who reports can also have another six people reporting to him (another team of seven) and on and on. Some leaders are able to oversee larger teams. The number of people one person can oversee is related to such factors as:

- The experience of the team members. Experienced staff members need less supervision while inexperienced members need more.
- The complexity of ministry. Complex ministries require more oversight while less complex ones require less oversight.
- The personal skills of the leader. Skillful leaders can manage more people while less skillful leaders can manage fewer people.
- The style of leadership. By coaching in groups one can oversee more people. When coaching one-on-one, the leader can oversee fewer people.
- The confidence of the leader. Secure leaders delegate more while insecure leaders do more work themselves.

Nurturing

Doran McCarty writes in *Working with People* that "a leader does not announce that a collection of people is a team."[7] Building a healthy staff team happens over time as the staff members focus on bonding, communicating, and supporting each other. "A team is not just any group working together. Committees, councils, and task forces are not necessarily teams. Groups do not become teams simply because someone labels them as a team."[8]

According to McCarty, a group of people becomes a team by wanting to be a team and working together. A team forms over time through shared goals and mutuality as team members turn to each other for information, help, and emotional support. You know a team has formed when what the staff achieves corporately becomes more important than the personal agenda of each member.[9]

◼ Steps to Nurturing a Healthy Staff

Do you remember the late night king of television, Johnny Carson? Viewers of Carson's show will remember the team relationship Johnny had with sidekick Ed McMahon and bandleader Doc Severinsen. Their team was purely professional, however—Johnny, Ed, and Doc would show up at a certain time, fulfill their roles, and then leave. They did not know each other outside of their professional relationship. That is not the way to build a healthy staff. Some have tried it and it eventually backfires.

Commenting on his observations during wartime conditions, General S. L. A. Marshall advised,

> It is . . . vital that an army should foster the closest acquaintance among its soldiers, that it should seek to create groups of friends, centered if possible on someone identified as a "natural" fighter, since it is their "mutual acquaintanceship" which will insure that no one flinches or shirks.[10]

How does a team develop a close acquaintance and become a group of friends? Most of the answer can be summarized in four words: training, travel, travail, and triumph. Eugene's story at the beginning of this chapter did not mention it, but his army buddies had trained together for several weeks and owned a similar philosophy of combat. They had traveled together on ships from the United States to England and from England to France, which afforded them hours of free time to talk about their past experiences and future dreams. Once in combat, they endured travails, such as the deaths of comrades, personal sickness, and lost battles. They experienced triumphs in battle that gave them hope for eventual victory. Taken together these experiences bonded them into a team that loved enough to die for each other.

The same principles that bonded Eugene's team during World War II form the foundation for nurturing staff teams today. Creating some similar experiences will nurture a close acquaintance among staff members resulting in a bond of friendship that means team members will serve each other sacrificially.

Spend Time with Staff

A leader nurtures a pastoral staff team when he encourages the team to spend time together. Four types of time together are needed by the average staff team member.

Meeting Time

Group time with staff alone is needed for sharing, planning, and study. The more we strategize, the more we harmonize is the basic principle. As a general rule, paid pastoral staff need at least one staff meeting a week together just for communication. A regular staff meeting provides for the sharing of reports and feedback on each team member's ministry. While this may sound like common sense, there are still a number of staff teams that rarely meet together. However, just meeting together in a weekly staff meeting cannot build a team.

Social Time

Group time with staff for worship, fun, and bonding is also needed. The more we pray and play together, the more we stay together is the basic principle. A social time at least once a quarter for the entire staff, and occasionally with their families, is a good practice. It is worth the investment to take the staff away at least once a year for a weekend of skiing, camping, or other recreational event. One pastor took his staff to a paint ball course where the entire team shot each other in a fun time of team play. Other pastors play games, such as golf or racquetball, with staff members.

Individual Time

Each staff member who reports directly to the senior pastor needs a minimum of one time per month with the senior pastor alone for work and sharing. This is a formal time of meeting for discussion of ministry and personal issues. Rather than always meeting in the senior pastor's office, it is wise to occasionally meet in the associate's office.

Individual Informal Time

Nurturing a healthy staff requires informal time for the senior pastor to get to know each staff member individually. Once a quarter, a senior pastor should take time to socialize with each staff member who reports directly to him. This can be a scheduled social time or something as unplanned as traveling together to another location. The important thing is that it be a time for building the relationship.

Communicate with Staff

The best teams communicate with each other. Communication is a major challenge for staff teams. In fact it is one of the struggles most often mentioned by staff members. At one of the largest churches in the United States, the senior pastor was known for working at home throughout the week. He communicated with his secretary and pastoral staff via e-mail and came into the office only on Sunday mornings. No time was spent in staff meetings or one-on-one relationships. Unfortunately the senior pastor's lack of nurturing his staff came back to haunt him, for when the board turned against him, none of the staff supported him. Healthy teams do not communicate just through e-mail or memos but pursue each other for face-to-face conversations.

Nothing can so quickly destroy a team's harmony and trust level as the withholding of pertinent information. The staff should be informed of the direction of the church "like the captain of a ship telling the crew where the boat is headed and what detours to expect and why."[11] Sometimes team members simply want to know what is going on in every area of the church ministry. This is impossible in a complex multiple staff environment. On the other hand, it is important that a staff member be kept informed about anything that will affect her sphere of ministry. *Remember: We are always down on what we are not up on.* Keep staff members in the formal flow of information. Build structures that allow staff to come to the person overseeing their work. Encourage one-on-one discussions between staff as well as structured meetings. Personal relationships breed trust. And effective communication can take place only among people who trust each other.

Establish expectations of mutual honesty. Appropriate self-disclosure by the team leader encourages openness and honesty from the team members. Trust between staff members is established when each agrees to share appropriate information openly. Confidentiality is another key ingredient that must be maintained. Share information and decision-making processes as much as possible.

Agree not to have to agree on everything. Pastor Melvin Amundson, speaking about feedback, suggests, "My door is always open and your suggestions are always welcome. I only ask that you use your ideas like seeds, not bullets. Plant them so they will grow, not wound."[12] The key is not to agree on everything but to listen, hear, and reflect on what is being said.

The best teams communicate with God. They spend time praying together about their mutual ministry and about the needs of team members. You will find them praying with each other in their offices as they live out their covenant of mutual teamwork.

Support the Staff

Insist on a minimum of one day off per week for each team member and set the example by taking yours. *Remember: In ministry, stretch becomes snap.* From time to time, release staff from Sunday morning or evening services to let them rest. These measures will prevent staleness and promote personal development.

Push for adequate vacation time and study leave and set the example by taking yours. As a rule, all full-time staff members should have a minimum of one month vacation per year. The long hours, emotional wear and tear, and twenty-four-hour on call nature of church ministry take their toll on all full-time staff members. Senior pastors, and those with schedules requiring unusually heavy mentoring or speaking, need six weeks to two months off each year.

Insist on the best possible benefits and working conditions for staff. George Bullard, national consultant with the South Carolina Baptist Convention, writes:

> Recruitment and retention of qualified staff is another hidden cost in the present crisis. Eagles will primarily go where they are called, but they will not make financial sacrifices that are too deep. Churches who expect sacrifices, or who cannot meet the perceived needs of staff, will not be able to attract and retain eagles.[13]

Leaders are providers. Thus whatever a leader's staff member needs to minister with excellence, a good leader will attempt to provide.

Publicly and privately hold staff in high esteem. Dr. McDowell advises, "Tell your congregation of your confidence in members of your staff. Report from the pulpit on the impact of their ministries."[14] Sprinkle compliments that will help your staff focus on the proper goals and direction. For example, a senior pastor might praise a worship pastor by saying, "That was an outstanding song. Let's all give him a hand." But a better approach, one that points in the right direction, would be to say something like, "Thank you for bringing us into the presence of God today. Because of your faithful use of your gifts, God was magnified in our worship service."

With a large staff, it is not possible to publicly acknowledge every pastor every Sunday. But going public with praise in appropriate and regular amounts will help each staff member sense that her ministry is worthwhile. Members of the congregation will give more respect to staff members who receive public praise from the senior pastor. Do not underestimate the value of a carefully handwritten note sent to an associate staff member. Most people who have been in ministry a number of years hold on to such expressions of thanks with much appreciation.

Be sensitive to the hurts of associate staff. The nature of church ministry means that pastoral staff go from moments of adulation to moments of rejection. In times of hurt and rejection, staff members need the sensitivity and compassion of a senior pastor to nurse them back to health. Minister to, not just through, the staff. One pastor shared, "I came to a staff meeting one day and shared that my wife was distressed about fleas that had invaded our home. The senior pastor recommended that I leave the staff meeting and go home to help. Later that day he came by our house and asked if there was anything he could do. My wife and I will never forget his caring attitude."

Be sure to demonstrate heartfelt appreciation to all staff members for their work and commitment. Peter Drucker states, "The first responsibility of a leader is to define reality. The last is to say thank you."[15]

Obstacles to Healthy Teams

1. *Conflict in personal values or style between team members.* This is the number one source of team division. Problems occur when a significant personal value of a teammate is not given priority.
2. *Seeking to fulfill personal significance through a ministry role.* Trouble lurks around the corner when a team member mixes his or her search for significance with role definition.
3. *"Misfiring" minister identity.* A person's ministry identity is a blend of two primary components: (a) spiritual gifts and (b) ministry burden or passion. Misfiring on either of these significant facets of God's design can create a loss of fruit and joy.

Adapted from Paul R. Ford, "The Harvest Is Plentiful, but the Laborers Are Arguing," *Church Smart Resources* 3, no. 3 (n.d.) 1–2.

Meeting Each Other's Needs

One of the advantages, and responsibilities, of serving on a pastoral staff is to care for the concerns of team members. Team members who understand each other's needs and work to meet those needs will find they develop a healthy relationship. Here are the main needs for staff members on a pastoral staff team.

Senior Pastor

Loyalty

The senior pastor needs loyalty. Here is how Karl Menninger defines loyalty:

Loyalty means not that I agree with everything you say or believe you are always right. Loyalty means that I share a common ideal with you and that, regardless of minor differences, we fight for it, shoulder to shoulder, confident in one another's good faith, constancy, and affection.[16]

The depth of confidence each team member has in the senior pastor is determined by several factors and exists at several levels:

Level A: The team member will die for the leader.

Level B: The team member will fight, but not die, for the leader.

Level C: The team member will not fight for the leader, but will not oppose the leader—loyalty is more institutional than personal.

Level D: The team member is a doubter.

Level E: The team member is an antagonist who seeks to erode, will fight against, and may even be willing to sacrifice the institution to "get at" the leader.[17]

Staff members need to be at level A or B for an effective team relationship to exist. If associate staff are at levels D or E, the results can be particularly devastating. At level E, senior pastors may criticize the staff but they will protect the church structure. Associate staff may assault the church structure to get at the senior pastor. In this sense associate pastors are more dangerous. Associate staff may be concerned with protecting their limited resources and ministries. Senior pastors tend to protect the total church.

Being Informed

As we have seen, an important part of being a team member is keeping each other informed. This is especially true for the team leader or senior pastor. The senior pastor needs clear communication. Staff members must share information about the church, people, and ministries so that the pastor is kept informed. Such communication must include patient listening so that misperceptions and misunderstandings are avoided. It is especially important that senior pastors be told about the bad stuff as well as the good stuff. *Remember: You are not doing the senior pastor a favor by shielding him from reality.*

The senior pastor needs no surprises. Timely communication avoids surprises—either good or bad. When good things happen, it is wise to make certain the senior pastor knows what took place so he is able to rejoice with you and others in the accomplishment. And the senior pastor must be kept informed of unfortunate happenings. If a senior pastor learns of a major problem from another source, it undermines the trusting relationship with the staff member who hesitated to inform him. While a staff member may think he is protecting the senior pastor by withholding difficult news, doing so only causes greater problems when the senior pastor discovers the truth on his own.

Recognition and Acceptance

The senior pastor needs recognition and acceptance. Most senior pastors believe they have been called to a public ministry. As such, they enjoy being in front of others. However, the public ministry leaves senior pastors exposed to much criticism. As someone has said, "The tallest tree catches the most wind." Besides criticism, the unrelenting pressures of ministry tend to bog down even the most committed leader. Senior pastors, especially, need to receive honest recognition and loving acceptance for faithful ministry. Michael Woodruff, a church consultant in Bellingham, Washington, advises:

> When you consider that it takes at least ten praises to balance one cut, you know that most senior pastors are functioning with a compliment deficit. A kind word from their staff members helps. Look for opportunities to build up your senior pastor.[18]

Staff Members

When pastoral staff team members are interviewed, seven general needs are often mentioned. Team members need:

1. To be taken seriously. Team members are often looked on as second-class pastors or gofers for the senior pastor. However, to do their ministry well, they need to be viewed as full-fledged pastors with serious ministries to lead.
2. Authority with their responsibility. Team members need to be released to do their jobs without someone looking over their shoulders. This implies having the necessary authority to make decisions within the constraints of the mission, philosophy, and policies of the church.
3. Open communication to people who make decisions in their areas of ministry. Team members must be able to talk with leaders who make policy decisions regarding their ministries. If team members are not on executive boards, they must be provided access to those who are on such boards to present plans and answer questions regarding their specific areas of ministry.
4. Honest affirmation. Team members need specific praise for a job well done. They look for honest praise of good ministry results.
5. To be supported openly. Team members need recognition and support from the senior pastor before the entire congregation. This validates their ministry and creates support throughout the entire body. Writing about this issue, Jerry Brown reminds us:

> This helps to correct the problem some people have of idolizing their pastor and treating other staff members as handmaidens. In some churches if the pastor does not express his affirmation of the staff member, some

church members will hesitate to follow that staff person's leadership.[19]

6. To be confronted in private. Team members need praise to be public and criticism to be private. To criticize a team member publicly will damage the fragile morale of the entire team.
7. Appropriate visibility. Team members need regular promotion of their individual ministries. In large churches promotion of each team member's individual ministry every week is not possible, but regular visibility is necessary to demonstrate the importance of each team member's role.

The nurturing of team ministry is an ongoing job. Occasionally the pressure of an expected or unexpected challenge will speed the process along, but in most situations developing a strong team takes time.

It is worth the effort to nurture the pastoral team. Those that work at it will find that the pastoral team on which they serve demonstrates the same characteristics of commitment as those found in Eugene Collins's unit in World War II. And they will find the members of the team love each other just as much too.

CHAPTER **EIGHT**

Motivating a Superior Staff

The path was worn and slippery. My foot slipped from
under me, knocking the other out of the way, but I
recovered and said to myself, "It's a slip and not a fall."

Abraham Lincoln

There is a new order today. Effective pastors recognize the
need for motivating their staffs collectively while remaining
sensitive to the professional and personal needs of individuals. The new order of team ministry means staff members
must be viewed differently. They are no longer employees
who can be told what to do, but volunteers who elect to serve
on a particular church staff. As such, all staff members
should be viewed as consultants.

The power has shifted from the employer to employee. The
focus is less on what the staff member can offer the church
and more on what the church can offer the staff worker. View-
ing staff members in this manner will help shape the church
environment to keep the staff members challenged, ener-
gized, and eager to come to work. Today's staff members have
strong individual beliefs and personalities. They respond bet-

ter to being pulled than being pushed. They need to know why something is being asked of them and they must have opportunity to digest, test, and challenge their assignments when necessary. Like skilled workers in other fields, they respond best when the team leader or senior pastor:

- Focuses on the ministry of each staff member by making their work challenging and exciting.
- Motivates staff members by offering them opportunities, challenges, and growth as both individuals and professionals.
- Treats all staff members as professional partners. As professionals, each staff member has studied and internalized a body of knowledge and experience that supersedes that of the congregation in which they minister. Therefore, their expertise should be respected. The effective leader supports them in the application of their expertise and helps them extend it further.
- Allows staff members to influence decisions that determine where and how their expertise is applied, as well as how it contributes to the overall church ministry.
- Respects the professional status and dignity of staff members.
- Minimizes burdens and obstacles to the accomplishment of the staff member's role.

◤◣ Motivating without a Gun

A famous bank robber, Willy Sutton, reportedly once said: "You can get further with a kind word and a gun than with a kind word alone." In the traditional bureaucratic church environment, staff members are often motivated by a controlling autocratic style of management not too far from what Willy Sutton envisioned. Staff members have very little say in their ministry assignments and serve at the pleasure of the senior pastor or board.

In today's environment the emphasis is on collaborative team ministry. Thus a team identity must be developed. This identity is a collective team understanding based on who the team thinks they are, not just on the senior pastor's pronouncement. Professional staff members desire to be part of a self-directed team. For this to be realized, the senior pastor or other team leader can no longer motivate the staff to do their best by bullying them, making all their decisions, treating them like children, or trying to intimidate them. The total top-down approach to management kills initiative, enthusiasm, creativity, and motivation.

While senior pastors are focused on the big picture, they need people they can depend on to keep an eye on the details—tending to the day-to-day requirements of running the church ministry. However, when staff members dislike their roles or are indifferent toward them, their attitudes lead to high turnover, poor ministry, and low productivity.

The key to motivation in the twenty-first century is involvement. As a rule, the closer staff members feel to the church ministry, the more likely they will feel good about themselves and their roles and be eager to work in harmony. Involvement of the staff team requires five major sources of motivation—five factors or questions that every staff member consciously or unconsciously asks:

- Why are we here?—mission
- Where am I going?—goals
- How am I doing?—feedback
- What's in it for me?—rewards
- What happens when I need help?—support

Motivating staff in today's team environment is most effective when these five issues are addressed.

◄▪ Mission—Why Are We Here?

Superior motivation occurs when staff members embrace and celebrate a common mission. If staff members do not understand the overall mission of the church, they will not know how their ministry contributes to it. When staff members understand the church's mission, they will be motivated to tie their personal ministry to the corporate mission. Staff members need to find meaning in their work just as they do in their personal lives. The more clearly a staff member recognizes how her ministry directly ties into the larger mission of the church, the more motivated she will be.

The first step in using this key to motivate staff members is to define the mission. A church's mission (or purpose) is its reason for being and must be developed with the input of staff members. Nationally known church consultant Dr. R. Daniel Reeves believes that team ministry involves "ownership and self-initiated vision in which members carry out plans they themselves have conceived or have had a part in conceptualizing."[1]

The second step is to communicate how the corporate mission relates directly to the staff member's ministry area. Each individual team member must be involved in the process of determining how he fits into the corporate mission. The less time a team leader spends discussing the mission of the church with his staff, the more likely the staff will focus on something else to the detriment of the team and the church.

◄▪ Goals—Where Am I Going?

At all levels, responsibility motivates. It is important to allow staff to set their own agendas and goals, thereby taking on responsibility. Staff members will only be motivated to help fulfill the corporate mission when each individual's goals are tied to that mission. Motivated staff members have questions and ideas, and it is in the interest of the senior pastor, or other team leader, to hear them out and encourage more, even if their thoughts are not always doable.

The process for setting goals must be taken seriously. In today's decentralized team atmosphere, leaders should meet with each team member who reports directly to them. The leader begins by asking each staff member to set individual ministry, personal, and family goals. Setting family goals may seem strange at first, but the team member's family must be cared for if the team member is to be emotionally able to function well in a team setting. In fact the best predictor of whether a teammate stays at the church is whether her family is happy.

The more staff members decide for themselves what their goals are, the greater the chance they will work at high levels of productivity. Work hard at establishing standards and determining accountabilities. It is what is called "high-involvement planning." Each staff member decides together with the team leader what expectations will be for the coming year. Goals should be realistic, understandable, measurable, behavioral, and attainable. Quantify each goal as much as possible so it will be easier to evaluate success at the end of the year. If a goal cannot be quantified, define as clearly as possible what the contribution is and how it affects the ministry of the church.

By the time the goal-setting process is finished, staff persons should know exactly what responsibilities and accountabilities they have for the coming year. Have staff members sign off on their individual plans, not only as individuals taking responsibility for their part but also as members of the team with mutual goals. The final set of goals must not be simply the team leader's goals, but the goals of the individual staff members. *Remember: Increasing the team member's responsibility for her own ministry translates directly into greater ministry satisfaction and a heightened sense of motivation and loyalty to the team.*

After all team members have established their own set of goals, schedule a staff meeting during which each member will share his goals with the total team. This brings team accountabilities into play and provides opportunity for team-mates to further shape the goals. For instance, if a team member's goals do not leave time for his family, the entire team can point this out, thereby providing a balanced accountability. After this meeting, it is best to leave well enough alone for at least three months. But each quarter another staff team meeting can be devoted to updates on each team member's progress. Reporting to the entire team is a stronger motivator than simply reporting to the team leader. It also allows the entire team to keep a close watch on how the ministry is going. At each meeting the team leader must watch, listen, and solicit opinion, but generally the team leader should let the team take any needed action. For example, when a team member consistently fails to perform or follow through on responsibilities, the entire team will point it out and call for change.

◥ Feedback—How Am I Doing?

Staff members may have the best of intentions of reaching their goals but they will often find it difficult to stay on track. One of the best ways to help them stay motivated to reach their goals is to provide feedback—frequent, accurate, useable, neutral information they must know if they are going to do their ministry task well.

Feedback is different from reinforcement. Feedback is neutral while reinforcement implies a value judgment. Giving rewards (see below) provides reinforcement. What motivates professional staff is feedback through neutral means, such as statistics, charts, and graphs, which assist each staff member in evaluating her ministry.

Do Performance Reviews Right

There is only one good reason for having annual performance reviews: to hold people accountable for the commitments they make to the other members of the staff team. Senior pastors and other team leaders find it difficult to do performance reviews. While performance reviews take place typically once a year, it is wise to meet at least quarterly. In some situations it may be necessary to meet monthly or even weekly. Begin by asking a staff member to evaluate his current progress toward reaching his goals. After he has finished, offer your own analysis. Provide whatever encouragement, discipline, support, training, or coaching is needed to make the staff member successful.

Staff members tend to react positively to positive direction. When doing performance reviews, keep in mind that there is a difference between criticism and correction. Correction encourages; criticism discourages. Try to make your comments corrective rather than critical. For example, saying, "You normally listen better than that" is better than saying, "You can't take criticism." And, "You can do better than that" is better than "I'm getting tired of your lousy work." Performance reviews are difficult but the long-term effects on the staff members and the church ministry is worth the effort.

Understand the Importance of Peers

Professional workers are sensitive to the praise they receive from their peers. The input of a staff member's peers has a much stronger impact on the staff member's motivation than the input of the senior pastor alone. There are ways, however, for the senior pastor to encourage team members to praise each other. For example, at a staff meeting, he can ask each person to share a positive comment about another team member.

Much peer reinforcement takes place today through informal networking, inside and outside the worker's own church. Networking allows a staff member to use the ministries of others as a benchmark for evaluating her own ministry and assessing how well she is doing. It also provides a clear picture of how her church is doing in keeping abreast of new ministry agendas.

Refresh the Context of Ministry

A wise senior pastor will provide regular confirmation that each staff member's ministry is valued. Associate staff members tend to put their heads down and work hard at their projects. When they do come up for air, however, they look for encouragement that their work is needed. And they want to know what is coming next. So keep them informed about future directions. If they do not receive confirmation of their ministry value and an indication of overall direction, they may lose energy. The trick is to always maintain a clear context for current ministry and for future direction.

◤ Rewards—What's in It for Me?

Major concerns in motivating staff members include how much, how often, and how to fairly reward each person for his work. Rewards fall into two basic categories: intangible (social) and tangible (economic). Both are valuable to maintain proper motivation. As already noted, one of the most effective motivators for staff members is the expression of praise for specific accomplishments. Public praise and position titles such as "executive pastor" can be significant motivators, particularly if awarded by the staff team. Surveys of workers in many fields consistently report that 50 to 60 percent of them never receive a verbal or written thank-you for a job well done. This may explain why so many workers are dissatisfied and lack motivation. Senior pastors or team leaders will want to try various types of rewards to motivate their staffs.

Showcase Contributions

What really motivates staff members in the twenty-first century is pride in accomplishment. Staff members crave and thrive on recognition of their contributions to the ministry. For some, public recognition is important; for others, appreciation needs to be offered in private. The ways workers are rewarded should be tailored to their individual needs.

Pastor Rick Warren recommends "When you are with your staff, give more strokes than pokes."[2] Jerry Brown, writing in *Church Staff Teams That Win,* advises, "Occasionally, public recognition of a staff member's faithfulness and work should be given. This provides the opportunity for the whole church family to affirm the individual staff member."[3]

Kenneth Blanchard and Spencer Johnson offer seven ways to praise effectively:

1. Tell people up front that you are going to let them know how they are doing.
2. Praise people immediately.
3. Tell people what they did right—be specific.
4. Tell people how good you feel about what they did right and how it helps the organization and the other people who were there.
5. Stop for a moment of silence to let them "feel" how good you feel.
6. Encourage them to do more of the same.
7. Shake hands or touch people in a way that makes it clear that you support their success in the organization.[4]

Reward Collective Accomplishment

I have already talked about the importance of a team leader's spending time with the team. It is a powerful investment in the future of the church and goes a long way in showing the team your appreciation of their accomplishments. Reward the accomplishments of the team by doing something special with them, such as going out for dinner or taking them on a fun outing. You may want to keep the activity a surprise. About one week ahead tell the staff to keep one day free the following week. When that free day arrives, lead them on a trip to a museum, an amusement park, or other fun outing as a reward for a job well done. Pay for everything on the trip. Be creative and you will think of many exciting ways to reward the entire staff together. Effective churches in the twenty-first century will have a culture that shows staff members they are appreciated and senior pastors who "mean it and believe it" when they say thank you.

Share the Wealth

Pay staff well. When pastoral staff are paid well, it heightens energy and pushes creativity since they do not worry about making ends meet financially. Sharing the wealth eliminates the resentment, lack of motivation, and turnover that frequently occur when the senior pastor receives an ever-increasing paycheck and the staff does much of the detailed work. Getting more money is not the total picture. As a general rule, staff members choose to stay where the work environment is value-centered, collegial, creative, and responsive. However, consistent low pay has an impact on the level of motivation of staff.

Sharing the wealth does not always mean a salary increase. It can be done in creative ways that will build loyalty and motivate staff members. Pastor David Andersen shared the following story of how his senior pastor had shared the wealth with his staff and molded them into a motivated team.

> Shortly after I began work at Baptist Temple, Dr. Wilkes showed me a small, metal cash box. He explained that the money in the box was from wedding fees and speaking engagements paid to himself, the other associate minister, and the minister of music. Each minister on the staff contributed all fees received, and twice a year the money was equally distributed among all.
>
> Dr. Wilkes had initiated the system and was the largest contributor. I was the newest member on the staff, and I

knew I would seldom be contributing to the fund, but I soon realized that this was one way Dr. Wilkes sought to equalize our relationship.

He explained to me that because of the nature of our different responsibilities, we could not all contribute equally to the fund; work of one enabled the others to have more freedom for outside engagements.

After I thanked Dr. Wilkes and got up to leave, he handed me an envelope. Inside was *my* share from the cash box for the past six months. I had been on the staff for only one month!

With this type of equality and sharing I quickly felt myself to be a part of a team. Staff meetings involved maximum participation. I *wanted* to do a good job. I *wanted* to see things happen. I *wanted* to share ideas, and I felt the openness for this to happen.[5]

Let Staff Be Winners

Staff members find they enjoy working, and are most productive, where they are appreciated. Ted Engstrom and Ed Dayton suggest team leaders use the following appreciation checklist as a way to remember to show appreciation to team members.[6]

1. I have written a personal note of appreciation to a staff member this week.
2. I usually remember people's birthdays.
3. I know how long each person reporting to me has been with the organization.
4. I have discussed a personal problem with a staff member in the last two weeks.
5. I discuss personal performances with each of my staff members at least once a year.
6. I have thought about and have goals for the personal growth of those reporting to me.
7. I have had lunch with a member of my staff in the last week.

8. Our organization is continuously analyzing cost of living against present salaries.
9. We supply training opportunities to qualified staff.

People join a staff for the psychic income, not just the monetary income. While there may be economic restraints on what a staff member can be paid, there are no restraints on the recognition they can be given. Peter Drucker believes:

> The leaders who work most effectively, it seems to me, never say "I." And that's not because they have trained themselves not to say "I." They don't think "I." They think "we"; they think "team." They understand their job to be to make the team function. They accept the responsibility and don't sidestep it, but "we" get the credit.[7]

In their highly respected book *In Search of Excellence,* Thomas Peters and Robert Waterman Jr. determined that one of the insights all organizations can learn from excellent companies is that most of their people are made to feel that they are winners.[8] Staff members tend to act in accordance with their image of themselves. If they see themselves as well regarded, they will try to perpetuate this image. This is where a supportive team leader comes in. Praise, appreciation, respect, new challenges, bonuses, raises—all these are rewards that help staff members know they are winners.

⚏ Support—What Happens When I Need Help?

Even highly trained, professional, and motivated staff members need help in ministry.

Pay Respect

An atmosphere of respect is widely considered by professionals as necessary for a happy and productive staff team.

Studies by human resource firms have found that conveying respect and value is an effective way to motivate and retain staff members in any field of work. While this seems simple, failure to show respect to staff members is surprisingly common and is one of the complaints expressed by associate staff concerning their senior pastor. A lack of respect diminishes a staff member's willingness to participate, but being respected motivates her to work harder. "Nothing stimulates enthusiastic cooperation more than the sense of individual belongingness, acceptance, and uniqueness."[9]

Provide a Steady Flow of Up-to-Date Information

In a rapidly changing ministry, up-to-date information is essential for effectiveness. Keeping current must transcend church boundaries. Staff members should be given permission to contact anyone who may help in this endeavor, whether inside or outside the church. John C. Maxwell, an authority on leadership, recommends that leaders "communicate with everyone. Don't be a fact hog. Share information with everyone who is affected, not just with the key players."[10]

Provide the Best Resources

Unlike yesteryear's ministry, when staff members took what resources you gave them, today's staff members know what is available and want the best resources possible. By providing associate staff members with up-to-date tools—cell phones, computers, pagers, e-mail, Web sites, and video equipment—their ministries will be enhanced and they will be happier.

Keep Hierarchy in Check

Staff members in the twenty-first century are impatient with bureaucracy, too many meetings, and senior pastors who tell them too often what they have to do. All these things violate their professional expertise and individual ability. Rather than focusing on who's in charge, it is better to define what needs to be accomplished to reach the vision. Then release the staff member to develop his own team to complete a portion of the task, leaving him responsible for goals, schedules, and accountabilities. The underlying premise is that staff members want freedom and responsibility in their defined area.

When staff members perceive that bureaucratic management is consuming their time and energy, productivity will plummet. Thus it is best to stay away from elaborate documentation, such as lengthy written reports. Keep meetings short, on target, and well defined.

Remove Obstacles

Professional staff members want to focus on their ministry, and anything a senior pastor can do to remove extraneous barriers, interruptions, and bureaucracy is appreciated. This includes being allowed to break some of the rules once in a while. Mindlessly adhering to policies or following traditional practices undermine the morale and enthusiasm of staff members. From time to time, staff members need to feel they can break the rules without being chewed out, demoted, or dismissed. Doing what is right for the mission is more important than following the rules.

Provide Challenging Work

The professional staff member's true calling is the ministry itself. If forced to choose between challenging ministry in an average environment or mundane work in a terrific environment, most will choose the challenging work.

Make Success Everyone's Job

There is no more frustrating experience than asking someone for help and having them say, "That's not my job." In a team ministry atmosphere, everyone is responsible for the success of the team. The senior pastor must set the example by going out of his way to help other staff members. By serving outside of his box, the senior pastor demonstrates the value of serving for the good of the team.

◤ Measuring Motivation

It is interesting that many senior pastors believe it is important to measure the morale of the congregation but ignore the motivation of the pastoral staff. What gets measured is taken seriously. If staff motivation is not measured, it winds up being taken for granted. By not focusing on staff motivation, problems are allowed to grow and opportunities to handle difficulties are missed.

The challenge, of course, is to figure out how to measure motivation. For most leaders, motivation is measured by gut feelings. Intuition can be a valuable resource, but it is better if motivation can be measured specifically.

One effective way to measure motivation is to develop a small questionnaire that asks questions such as:

- At church, do my opinions count?
- In the past six months has someone spoken to me about my personal development?
- Are my concerns taken seriously?

Low motivation is often caused by many small problems that can be eliminated quickly and inexpensively by bringing them to the surface and focusing on them. But little problems are easy to miss in the larger picture. The larger a church becomes, the more important it is that good systems be put in place for doing ministry. The danger is that after a while it is easy to stop thinking about the issues and the people involved. It is easy to forget to check up on them and to ask if the systems are serving their original purpose.

The only way to avoid missing the small problems is to conduct regular audits to take the pulse of the staff, find out how people are feeling, and check how things are going. An audit of motivation should be completed at minimum once a year, and every six months is best. Always ask staff members, What can we do differently?

There are, of course, subtle signs of low motivation. Here are some of the more common indicators that staff members are unmotivated.

- Staff members do not participate actively in staff meetings.
- Staff members display no creativity or innovation.
- Staff members form cliques.
- Staff members are in a hurry to leave, rather than hanging around to talk.
- Staff members rarely smile, laugh, or participate together in fun activities.
- Staff members shut you (the leader) out of their personal lives.
- Staff members do not feel comfortable coming to your office.
- Staff turnover is high.

Motivation is an intangible that affects staff members' attitudes and performance. A fun and relaxed atmosphere seems to be the ticket for most staff members today. When staff members stick around and talk to each other, it is a clear sign that morale is high.

In the final analysis, "The key ingredient in most successful projects is loving what you do. Having a goal or a plan is not enough. Academic preparation is not enough. Prior experience is not enough. Pleasure and productivity are Siamese twins in these unconventional times."[11]

CHAPTER NINE

Discipling Up

A multiple ministry is not a problem to be solved but an adventure to be lived.

Martin Anderson

"The meeting sure went a long time today. It just seemed like we kept getting off the subject. Did you sense it?" asked Sally Withers, the newly installed associate pastor of education at New Life Community Church.

"I did and it bothered me too," Dr. Launstein nodded in agreement. "This is one of the most complicated decisions I've faced in my eleven years as senior pastor. We've got a deadline to make the decision about camp this summer and I'm not sure it's going to get done."

"You know," Sally continued, "building consensus happens to be an interest of mine. I spent some time in school studying methods to achieve it."

"Is that so?" Dr. Launstein looked up in surprise. "Is there anything you'd like to pass on?"

Seeing Dr. Launstein's openness, Sally quickly spoke up, "Well, the first thing is to develop a clear agenda and stick to it. Then it's wise to develop clear alternatives that people can evaluate. If you'd like, I could draw up an agenda for next week's meeting and three alternatives based on the comments people made today."

"Good. Good! That would be very helpful." Dr. Launstein seemed honestly happy to get some help on the pending decision.

"Why don't I put together a draft and come to your office on Thursday so we can discuss the possibilities before next week?" Sally asked.

"Great! Thanks for bringing this up. It'll be a great help. See you on Thursday," Dr. Launstein confirmed as he headed for his office.

The conversation between Dr. Launstein and Sally Withers illustrates two aspects of staff ministry. First, everyone reports to someone else. Everyone has a boss, even in team ministry situations. Being the newest staff member at New Life Community Church, Sally knew she was to report directly to the senior pastor, Dr. Launstein. This, of course, is not surprising. What may be surprising is that the conversation also illustrates a second, lesser known fact of successful team ministry—associate staff must disciple up.

Sally understood that her success depended on discipling her senior pastor. During the staff meeting she had observed how frustrated Dr. Launstein became with the decision-making process and later she took charge of the relationship by volunteering to set the agenda and search out alternatives for the next meeting. By discipling her boss in this way, she helped him succeed, as well as establishing herself as a contributor to the total team ministry.

At first thought, discipling one's senior pastor or immediate supervisor does not seem logical. They are supposed to disciple the staff members not the other way around—at least that is the way team ministry has always been perceived. It is true, of course, that associate staff do not supervise the senior pastor. Associate staff do not normally conduct performance reviews of the senior pastor or assign work to the senior pastor or fire the senior pastor. Even in a flat collaborative team structure, where most hierarchical structures have been eliminated, the senior pastor occupies a stronger position of oversight than do other staff members.

However, team members do influence the senior staff member in many ways. Bob Mezoff, president of ODT Associates, a consulting firm that specializes in teaching people how to manage their boss, believes "You can't change 75 percent of what your boss does, but you can change 25 percent."[1] Discipling the senior staff member in that 25 percent area can add immeasurably to the success of the staff team's overall ministry. As church leaders move away from the old hierarchical command-and-control style of leadership to a consensus team style of ministry, the senior pastor–associate pastor relationship is becoming more of a two-way street with power and influence flowing in both directions. The key word in staff relationships today is "interdependence." In the complex world of twenty-first–century church life, all staff members must exert some degree of independence and initiative while at the same time maintaining a measure of interdependence on each other.

⬛ Why Disciple Your Senior Pastor

The most obvious reason to disciple your senior pastor is that the success of an associate's ministry is closely linked to that of the senior pastor. While it is possible for associate pastors to serve with skill and competence in their individual areas of ministry, the ultimate effectiveness of their ministry is strongly influenced by that of the senior pastor. Good performance of associate staff does speak for itself in many ways, but without a senior pastor who faithfully works out the larger relationships, associate staff never will reach their highest potential. It is rare to find exceptionally effective staff teams without a senior pastor who:

- Casts a common vision for the church and staff team
- Supports each staff member with training and resources to do the job
- Shepherds each staff member with love and care
- Serves the needs and concerns of each staff member
- Monitors each staff member's personal growth and development

Associate pastors cannot function well in their individual ministry areas without a strong relationship with the senior pastor. Associate staff need the confidence of the senior pastor to receive the resources and support necessary to do their jobs. There is always a new program to be developed, budget increase to be defended, or a facility improvement to be approved. Thus it is crucial that associate staff learn to disciple their senior pastor so he can be as effective as possible. As the senior pastor grows and develops in his area of ministry, associate staff members will be drawn along in his wake.

Another reason to disciple one's senior pastor is the fact that an associate's job is often dependent on the senior pastor. In most churches, when a senior pastor moves to another church, all associate positions are automatically up for review. There is no guarantee that a new senior pastor will choose to keep the current staff members. Thus it benefits the associate staff to make their senior pastor as effective as possible so that he continues to serve in the present church for as long as God wills.

Last, an inability to work with the senior pastor may affect one's health and happiness. A major reason that staff members experience frustration, depression, and some health problems is an inability to get along with the senior pastor. Discipling the senior pastor can make one's present ministry much more pleasant. No one is likely to serve your interests better than a supportive senior pastor.

▟ How to Disciple Your Senior Pastor

Here are some practical suggestions for discipling the senior pastor.

Learn What Makes the Senior Pastor Tick

The more you know about your senior pastor, the more effective you will be in discipling up. Michael Woodruff suggests all associate pastors should answer the following questions about their senior pastor.

> Does he make his best decisions in the morning or in the afternoon? On Monday or on Friday? What does she love to do? What does she hate? When is the worst time to meet with him? When is the best time to request additional funding? If you don't know the answers to these questions, then you are not as smart as you think you are.[2]

Try to learn as much about the person you report to as possible. In addition to the questions noted above ask:

- What is your senior pastor's geographic, educational, and professional background?
- How long has he been at this church, and in what capacities has he served?
- What about work habits? Is he a morning person or an afternoon person or a night person?
- What are his career goals, hopes, and dreams?

- What is the senior pastor's office like? What style of furniture has he chosen? What pictures and mementos are displayed?

Do not be too hasty in drawing conclusions, but knowing the answers to many of these questions can reveal much about how to work with the senior pastor.

Listen to Your Senior Pastor

One of the keys to successful relations with our family members, friends, and ministry team members lies in listening to what they have to say. No staff member can hope to serve well with a senior pastor, let alone disciple him, unless she is prepared to listen carefully to what he has to say.

As an associate staff member, you must listen actively to hear not just what the senior pastor says, but what he implies. Listen to what is being said and what is being omitted. Stay alert for key words, voice inflections, body language, or other codes that reveal what is going on behind the words themselves. Remember:

> Interpreting and acting on what your superior wants, and needs, rather than what you believe the organization wants and needs, has some very practical and important consequences. First, it keeps the lines of responsibility clear. Second, it makes communication much simpler. Third, it keeps loyalties from becoming divided. The result is a much more effective organization and much happier staff members.[3]

Keep Your Senior Pastor Informed

I come back to this important issue of communication. In good times and in bad times it is imperative that you keep your senior pastor informed. In fact the worse the news or the bigger the church, the more important it is that you make sure the pastor knows what is going on in your area of ministry.

Effective senior pastors thrive on information and respect associate staff members who can supply it. Nothing is more appreciated than factual information that helps the senior pastor make better decisions. Therefore, one of the best ways to disciple your senior pastor is to dig up useful information—facts and figures—regarding decisions being considered. Often an associate finds that the best way to get a senior pastor to do something is to supply him with the right information. Be sure to keep alert for items in newspapers, journals, magazines, and other publications that may be of interest to the senior pastor. When you find something of interest to him, clip it or copy it and pass it on to him.

Speak and Write Concisely

All senior pastors find their time being controlled by meetings, phone calls, and everyday administrative details. With this in mind, associate staff must learn to communicate with brevity. One good way to communicate is to master the art of developing and delivering what is called an "elevator speech." Whenever you have an idea or request, work at condensing it down so that you could present it in one minute while riding in an elevator with your senior pastor. Doing this will allow you to maximize the opportunities you have to speak with your pastor. This does not mean you should jam a lot of facts and figures into a one-minute presentation, but only that you be selective and direct about what you say.

In written communication, conciseness and clarity should also rule. In most cases any written communication should be no longer than one page. If you must provide your senior pastor with a longer document, place a one-page summary of the document's highlights on top. A good way to improve your writing is to read aloud what you have written. If it sounds good, it will most likely read well. It is always helpful to show the senior pastor something rather than to simply tell him. This is especially true when an associate tries to get a new idea across to the senior team leader. Using charts, graphs, and other visual communication is always appropriate. *Remember: It has been said that there are no clear writers, only clear thinkers.* Thus writing concisely and briefly demonstrates your ability to think, which all senior pastors appreciate.

Knowing your senior pastor's decision-making style comes in handy when communicating. Action-oriented pastors tend to prefer spoken communication, while process-oriented pastors often prefer everything in writing so they can carefully review all information. To effectively disciple your senior pastor, be sure to communicate in the style he prefers.

Solve Your Own Problems

One of the most frustrating aspects of being a senior pastor is having staff members who cannot solve their own problems. Amazing numbers of people—staff and lay leaders—want to bring their problems to the senior pastor. So many in fact that most senior pastors could schedule meetings all day just to hear about the problems. Thus, generally speaking, it is wise if you can keep problems away from your senior pastor's office as much as possible. Resist any desire to let the pastor know the difficulties of your ministry if you are simply trying to impress him. Senior pastors appreciate staff members who are rarely overwhelmed with their tasks.

As mentioned earlier, senior pastors do not like surprises. Thus at times it is necessary to take problems to your senior pastor. There will be issues that involve authority or have implications beyond your influence. And yes, there will be times when you just need help. When you do come to your senior pastor with an issue of this sort, it is wise to frame it as a request for advice rather than ask for a solution. And, along with your question, always bring a minimum of three potential solutions. Bringing along some suggested solutions shows initiative and thinking on your part. If it is a major issue, it is best to present the senior pastor with a list of potential possibilities and then allow him to choose. Avoid the tendency to stack the list of potential options in your favor, as doing so may be viewed critically. Be ready with your elevator speech, if the senior pastor asks your opinion on which option is the best one.

Give Your Senior Pastor Options

Every associate staff member has ideas that he believes will improve his church's ministry. Four suggestions are in order for offering such ideas. *First,* carefully select the time and place to make your suggestions. It is generally best to offer ideas when your senior pastor is in a good mood, alone, and facing a problem related to your idea. *Second,* offer your idea in a way that causes the least amount of disturbance to your senior pastor's routine. This usually means offering to do most of the work in implementing your ideas yourself! *Third,* think through your idea from your senior pastor's point of view before bringing it up. The church of the twenty-first century is an intricate organism with many connected parts. Be sure to think through the larger ramifications of your idea for the entire church. By being alert to all that is going on in the life of your church, you will be able to serve yourself, your pastor, and your church well. *Fourth,* remember that a suggested improvement, no matter how well presented, conveys criticism, since it implies that something needs changing. Be sure your suggestion is crucial enough to risk inflicting your senior pastor's ego with pain.

Do What You Say You Will Do

Senior pastors do not expect perfection and they can usually adjust to shortcomings. However, the one thing senior pastors cannot do is adjust to uncertainty. If you say you will do something and then do not follow through, it will make the senior pastor doubt your reliability. So if you are given an assignment that you feel you cannot accomplish, it is far better to say so up front than to accept the assignment and fail to follow through on it. Lack of perfection is one thing; lack of reliability is another.

When you are given an assignment that is beyond your competence or knowledge, it is best to admit it and state directly what you need to learn in order to accomplish the task. At that point the senior pastor can choose to give the assignment to another staff member, provide training for you to learn the necessary skills or knowledge, or team you with another person. Do not be afraid to admit honest inadequacy.

When you make an honest commitment to do a task and then discover that you are unable to do it, alert the senior pastor as quickly as possible. It is generally poor advice to hold off telling him in the false hope that something may change. The sooner you tell the pastor, the better for all concerned. In the long run it is better to be known for making an honest mistake than to be known as one who cannot be relied on. By being up-front with your senior pastor, you are teaching him that you can be trusted, which will go a long way in gaining his support in future ministry.

Make Your Senior Pastor Successful

Ted Engstrom and Ed Dayton, both formerly of World Vision, refer to this aspect of staff ministry when they declare, "A primary task of each person in an organization is to make his or her boss successful."[4] This is a well-known and well-accepted strategy in discipling up because, whether you like it or not, you will surely be identified with your senior pastor. It is in your own self-interest, as well as that of the church, to lift your senior pastor up rather than tear him down. The following suggestions summarize the various ways of making your senior pastor successful.

Represent Your Senior Pastor Fairly

Your senior pastor is also human and is bound to have weaknesses and shortcomings. Talk about his abilities and try not to discuss his weaknesses. When you speak well of your senior pastor, you establish yourself in his eyes as someone who can be trusted as a valuable member of the team.

Try to Understand Him

What is your boss's style? People are different. How does he think? Why does he think that way? What does he do best? Is he a decision maker, a problem solver, or both?

Try to Do It His Way

Even if your way seems better, do it his way. One day he'll discover your way, if you're patient.

Keep Him Informed

Don't surprise your senior pastor. Tell him first about decisions you want him to make, next what problems you anticipate, and above all what you plan to do.

Give Him Alternatives

If you are asking for a decision, don't give your senior pastor an alternative of one. Think through acceptable alternatives. You'll be less disappointed and so will he.

Don't Embarrass Him

Experience has found it is always wise to make your senior pastor look good. This means letting him take credit for ideas you conceived or created, letting him do the talking, and letting him announce good news (while you may have to announce the bad news).

Make Your Pastor Feel Good

A senior pastor who is in a good mood is much more approachable. Therefore, smart associate pastors desire their senior pastor to be happy. While you will not want to use flattery, there are honorable ways to make your senior pastor happy. Listen to him when he talks, offer heartfelt thanks, relay favorable comments from others, emphasize the positive rather than the peril, and follow his model where appropriate.

Be Loyal to the Senior Pastor

One of the downfalls of associates in all fields of endeavor is betrayal of trust. Criticism, backbiting, and back stabbing all derail promising relationships and fruitful ministry. Disloyalty is problematic for at least five reasons. *First,* it is dishonorable. If a staff member continues to serve in a church while working against the senior pastor, she is living a lie. *Second,* it creates disrespect. An associate cannot help but lose everyone's respect if she speaks and acts one way before the senior pastor and another way behind his back.

Third, disloyalty breeds disloyalty. People who work in an organization take their cues on how to act from their immediate supervisors. If those serving under your leadership see you being disloyal to the pastor, it will be easier for them to be disloyal to you.

Fourth, disloyalty creates friction. Senior pastors have their own informal communication channels and they are sure to hear of your disloyalty from others. After learning of your true feelings, the senior pastor will lose trust in you, which will be reflected negatively in all future relationships.

Fifth, disloyalty leads to loss of influence. Perhaps the most tragic aspect of disloyalty is that the disloyal associate cannot disciple up. The senior pastor will listen to the insights and ideas of other more loyal associates while ignoring the comments and advice of the disloyal one. In any case, working for a senior pastor whom you are disloyal to creates stress, heartache, and frustration that is rarely conducive to a healthy team ministry.

▟ How to Choose a Senior Pastor Who's Right for You

Discipling up is much easier if you serve with a senior pastor with whom you are compatible. You may think you have very little choice in who your senior pastor will be. On reflection, however, it should be clear that all associate pastors exercise some choice over which senior pastor they will serve. Discipling up actually begins with the selection of a good senior pastor. As an associate, whenever you look for a new place of service, you are actually looking for a new senior pastor. You should take into account the senior pastor who comes with the church. Here are five essential qualities you should look for in a senior pastor.

First, look for a senior pastor who is decisive. A fearful, indecisive senior pastor who hems and haws, shying away from risks, is to be avoided at all costs. Those who have served with senior pastors who are indecisive describe it as "weaving your way through a minefield." Serving with a decisive, fairly predictable senior pastor allows you to know what to expect. When serving with an inconsistent and indecisive pastor, you never can be sure of what will happen. It should be noted that indecisive leaders always fear new ideas. Those who dislike new ideas often fear delegating, since it leaves things out of their control. So look for a senior pastor who is decisive and is willing to take prudent risk. At least you will know most of the time where you stand.

Second, look for a senior pastor whose mission, values, vision, goals, and objectives essentially match your own. An associate can sometimes adapt to a senior pastor's personality, methods, and procedures. But adapting to or trying to change a senior pastor's core mission, values, vision, goals, and objectives is another story. History demonstrates that almost all superior senior pastor–associate pastor relationships are marked by compatibility in these five areas.

Third, look for a senior pastor who desires church growth. Healthy senior pastors yearn for their church to grow. Of course, they may not always use the term "church growth." They may talk about a healthy church or a developing church or an expanding church. Yet whatever term they choose to use in talking about the church, there will be a desire for the church to move forward. If they desire their church to move forward, they will help you grow and develop also. Church growth pastors tend to avoid being locked into dead-end activities and ministries. Make certain you do not lock yourself in with a senior pastor who has no vision for the future.

Fourth, look for a senior pastor who has little turnover among his associate staff. If most of his associate staff stays with him, it is an indication he treats his staff well. Good senior pastors usually experience little staff turnover. The best senior pastors, however, are those who have seen a few of their staff members leave to assume other challenging positions. A pattern of regular, but not rapid, staff movement such as this often demonstrates a senior pastor who attracts, coaches, and develops excellent staff members. The worst senior pastors are those who experience heavy staff turnover.

Fifth, look for a senior pastor who possesses personal qualities that balance yours. Determine not only what the senior pastor can do for you in terms of training and coaching, but also what you can do for him. Discipling up is much easier when you can offer your senior pastor qualities that balance his shortcomings. Many of the best senior pastor–associate pastor relationships have been between people who appear to be opposites. Keeping this in mind, look for a senior pastor who is not too much like yourself. Some common areas of compatibility are necessary as previously mentioned, but a degree of difference can lead to a healthy staff relationship.

◤ General Suggestions

When choosing a senior pastor with whom you will serve, try to avoid a person who has an extreme desire to please. Such senior pastors are generally insecure and worry too much about being liked. While such pastors are mostly pleasant people, they may fail to protect the interests of their staff members because they are preoccupied with pleasing everyone else in the church also. Additionally, in their desire to please you, they may not always tell you everything you need to know to do your task well. By withholding unpleasant information from you, they may put your ministry at risk. Fear not, however, the senior pastor who is demanding. The best senior pastors to work with are often demanding and may actually give you little praise.

An associate pastor who has developed a specialized expertise in a given field, such as evangelism or Christian education, may look for a senior pastor with ability in the same arena. While there is nothing wrong with this approach, there may be some pitfalls. People who have developed expertise in a given field will, in most situations, feel threatened by any suggestions to do ministry in a different way. They may insist that you, as the associate, do everything their way. Failing to delegate meaningful aspects of the ministry to you, the senior pastor may relegate only routine tasks to you. So caution is called for when the senior pastor is an expert in the same field as you.

The ages of the senior pastor and associate staff member are sort of a two-edged sword. For example, on the positive side, an older senior pastor may look out for the associate's interests like a father watching over his child. But, on the negative side, this can lead to an overprotective attitude, which limits the associate's growth and development.

On the positive side, the older senior pastor has a wealth of experience. On the negative side, he may be resistant to change. Interestingly, one of the best staff arrangements tends to be that of a younger senior pastor and an older associate pastor. In such an arrangement, the younger senior pastor may provide the vision and energy for ministry while having the experience and patience of the older associate to balance out his youthful exuberance. This arrangement also has its potential downfalls, especially when a younger senior pastor finds it awkward to work with an associate staff member who is his parents' age. Having pastors of about the same age is likely to be a good match when it comes to similar ways of thinking and acting. But the disadvantage may be that they feel competitive with each other. All things considered, age is something that should be considered but not held rigidly as a factor in determining if you want to serve with a given pastor.

In the final analysis, the best sources for determining what a senior pastor is like are the associate pastors who have previously served with him. If possible, seek out the associate pastors who have served in the same position you are considering. Interview the previous associate pastors but remember that their responses will be colored by their own personalities as much as by the senior pastor they describe.

CHAPTER **TEN**

Managing Staff Conflicts

> You ought to think three times before leading or join-
> ing a staff. It is delightful and rewarding if relationships
> are healthy, and destructive and disappointing if they
> are not.
>
> Anonymous

"I was surprised at the lack of consensus. Were you?" Mary, the church's youth director, asked the senior pastor follow-ing a particularly contentious staff meeting.

"Yes—and concerned," Mike said, staring at the floor in dismay. "We've got to resolve this soon or we'll be in big trou-ble. I can't believe that two of my most trusted staff mem-bers could get into such an argument."

"I feel the same way. Actually I'm quite hurt because it's not right for Christians to act that way. If those two don't stop feuding, it's going to affect the entire staff and even spread to the board of elders," Mary said.

"That's true," Mike agreed. "I know that we don't always agree on our plans, but this seems to be going too far. The problem is I'm not sure if I should get involved or just wait and hope they will settle the differences themselves. I'm trying to think my way through this. I just hope it can be settled without leaving any scars."

Mike and Mary's conversation reveals at least three aspects of staff conflict. *First,* pastoral staff teams do have conflict. *Second,* people often have unrealistic expectations that staff teams will be conflict free. *Third,* leaders do not always know what to do with conflict when it arises.

◤◥ Basic Multiple Staff Problems

In the ministry world of the twenty-first century, team-based leadership is thought by some to be a miracle cure for what ails churches. Unfortunately what at first seems like a simple paradigm to implement, may become just another problem-filled approach to ministry. Speaking of team ministry, someone reportedly remarked, "A team is like having a baby tiger given to you at Christmas. It does a wonderful job of keeping the mice away for about twelve months, and then it starts to eat your kids!"

Most teams function well for a few months but then they encounter predictable staff issues that threaten to pull the team apart. Underlying all problems of team ministry is, of course, human nature. Team members are human beings with all the attendant characteristics. Thus senior pastors often talk about shared leadership but then revert to claiming the sandbox as their own by overcontrolling decision making. Associate pastors talk about equality of input but then refuse to share information with other staff members. Team members talk about the good of the team but end up arguing over who gets the credit for what the team produces.

While there are numerous problems that may be encountered, most fall into one of four major categories: motivational, communicational, organizational, and relational.

Motivational Problems

According to studies completed among different types of teams in various settings, the following are the "big three" motivational problems for teams.

Free Riding

Free riding is when team members are not carrying their share of the ministry workload. Team members may be sharing in the glory of being on the team and in the total team accomplishments, but they drop the ball in their own area of ministry. Other team members notice the failure of their teammate to accomplish the task but do not want to tattle on him and thus harbor ill feelings for the poorly performing member.

There are two ways to approach free riding. *First,* the team leader must assist team members in setting specific goals and then must hold each team member accountable for accomplishing them. At a minimum, an associate who is free riding should be required to set quarterly goals and then meet with the team leader every quarter to report on which goals have been accomplished. *Second,* the team together must hold each other accountable for contributing to the team. The team must have the courage to confront each other in the total team environment and not let any team member get away with free riding.

Groupthink

Groupthink is when everyone on the team appears to think alike; no one raises objections or concerns about anything. Groupthink normally occurs when the group is very homogeneous and everyone does think alike; team members are close friends and no one wants to challenge their friends; or members are afraid and do not want to rock the boat.

If groupthink is a problem within a team, use one of the following two approaches. *First,* appoint a "devil's advocate"

153

every time the team meets. The devil's advocate role is to raise and investigate potential pitfalls in the team's thinking. This role should be rotated so that no one person is always the bad guy. *Second,* when the team meets, the senior pastor or team leader needs to share his opinions last after everyone else has had opportunity to comment on an issue. In group-think situations, team members will simply pick up on what the senior pastor wants and echo those sentiments in their own comments. By withholding comment early on, the team leader encourages freer thinking by all team members.

Social Loafing

Social loafing occurs when everyone knows about a problem but no one wants to be the first to mention it. Each team member feels that someone else will bring the problem before the group, but the result of social loafing may be that a problem is never noted or perhaps is mentioned too late to be properly addressed. To encourage responsibility, a senior pastor must communicate that all team members are to be honest and forthcoming, and, when someone does mention a difficult issue, he must not shoot the messenger.

Communicational Problems

Harold J. Westing, author and consultant on multiple-staff ministry, reports that the lack of communication and misunderstood communication rank first and second among items that lead to dissatisfaction among team members.[1] Two key communicational problems are commonplace among teams of all types: *Team members communicate very little with each other and team members communicate in harmful ways.*

Lack of Communication among Team Members

People who work together are not always personal friends. Indeed, some individuals find they can minister together quite competently without socializing much away from work. The way staff members feel about each other need not be a matter of great concern, unless it gets out of hand. What is out of hand? Staff relationships are out of hand if the following situations exist:

- Key staffers are not speaking to each other.
- Hostile camps have formed.
- Working together on projects happens only among team members who are friendly with each other.
- Staff members resist assignments outside their normal roles.
- Key information is held by a small subgroup and not shared with others outside the group.

There are situations where nothing the senior pastor can do will help. In such situations, it is best to let the feuding staff members work it out for themselves, provided the ministry is getting done and their difficulties are not counterproductive to the team. However, when counterproductive situations exist in a staff team, it is time to intervene. Here are a few suggestions to get started.

- Make the message clear that you want team members to cooperate. Such a message is most often heeded if hostilities are not widespread, but limited to a small group of two or three people. Consider holding a small and pleasant meeting to discuss the problem.
- Give attention equally to all those involved so no one will feel that you are taking sides. Along with your previous communication this will help make your point.
- Tell the team directly what you want. Many times it is best to sit down with the feuding team members and give them specific direction. Share with them how their

animosity is hampering the ministry of the group. Offer whatever is needed to iron out the problem.

- Manage difficult team members as a team rather than alone. Reframe any problems from a senior pastor–associate pastor problem to a team problem. Get the associate's peers involved, since letting the team down has a greater impact than letting the senior pastor down.
- Identify a common cause or purpose for everyone to work on together. Feuding may take place when no common sense of direction has been defined.
- Realign the roles of staff members so that individuals must cooperate in order to accomplish their objectives. Or, if you believe that working together is impossible, you could find ways to make the work autonomous or as little dependent on each other as possible. However, doing so would obviously defeat the purpose of a team ministry.

Harmful Communication

Harmful communication may become a silent epidemic as team members regularly spread malicious rumors, become involved in back stabbing, or simply give each other the silent treatment. This rude behavior goes by various names: workplace incivility, psychological aggression, hostile work environment, or workplace bullying.

A formal study on team problems in secular workplaces sheds light on the issues. Joel J. Neuman, director of the Center for Applied Management, lists the top ten acts of workplace bullying:

- Talking about someone behind her back
- Interrupting others when they are speaking or working
- Flaunting status or authority; acting in a condescending manner
- Belittling someone's opinion to others

- Failing to return phone calls or respond to memos
- Giving others the silent treatment
- Insults, yelling, and shouting
- Verbal forms of sexual harassment
- Staring, dirty looks, or other negative eye contact
- Intentionally damning with faint praise[2]

Unfortunately those who have served on a multiple staff can identify with at least eight of the ten items listed above. While such a hostile ministry environment is clearly unbiblical, it also leads to a tremendous amount of team ineffectiveness. Hostile team situations are very harmful to the individual and the church. Team members who have served in such negative situations report that they lost time worrying about avoiding the instigator and about future interactions. Their commitment to the church declined and it became difficult to give 100 percent effort to their task. At least half gave serious thought to resigning their positions and between 10 and 20 percent did resign to get away from the difficult work experience. People who have served in difficult team situations can also remember experiencing anxiety, sleeplessness, headaches, and low self-esteem.

As Christians we have been taught to believe that it is best to tolerate the problems and hope they will go away. During such experiences, a person's prayer life may get richer, but that is about all. To protect the team from such negative forms of communication, preventative and proactive measures must be used. *First,* the key is for the team leader to establish a gracious and loving atmosphere. How the team leader, or senior pastor, treats others sets the tone for the entire team. *Second,* the team as a whole must establish acceptable guidelines for personal communication. A good way is to have the team members establish a covenant under which they all agree to work.

157

Such a covenant should include comments on how team members will communicate with each other. *Third,* the team must commit to confronting those who violate the covenant.

Organizational Problems

Some team conflicts are attributable to organizational or management issues. Three of the most common are an overly controlling senior pastor, misunderstanding team roles, and inequity in salary.

Overly Controlling

Giving a staff member responsibility and letting him do the job is something that senior pastors or team leaders seem to have trouble doing. They don't know how to delegate. For one reason or another, they take on all the big ministry projects themselves. When they do hand off goals and assignments to a staff member, they hover over the staff member, constantly checking and rechecking, giving directions, making changes, and generally running the show. While the task may get done, neither the senior pastor nor associate gains very much.

Not letting go is a tendency of senior pastors who do not understand how crucial it is to their own growth to have a staff team that is capable of doing a larger job. If there have been times when you have added an important project to your own busy schedule, instead of letting a qualified associate do it alone, ask yourself the following:

- What am I afraid of? Leaders will often come up with what they believe are logical explanations of why they keep control. Some will say, "She won't get it done on time" or "He will make a mistake" or "I can do it faster." Unfortunately explanations of this sort are based on the fear of letting go and losing control. Determine to ask yourself what you are afraid of and then ask:

- What have I got to lose? At times you may have a great deal to lose and other times very little, depending on the nature of the assignment. In cases where you have a lot to lose, you can still delegate the task to an associate if you clearly communicate what needs to be done, build in deadlines, and make yourself available to provide assistance if necessary. Then, ask yourself:
- What have I got to gain? In most situations there is a lot to gain by delegating authority. You can lift a burden from your shoulders, help develop an associate staff member's skills and confidence, and pave the way for great success in the future.

Misunderstanding Team Roles

Role and title misunderstandings are quite common among members of multiple staffs. For example, is there a difference between a minister of music, a director of music, and a worship leader? If so, what are the differences and what does this mean to the team? What do the terms *associate, assistant,* and *director* indicate? How do such terms impact authority, responsibility, and accountability? Misunderstanding also surfaces regarding roles. For example, a question may come up as to who oversees the ushers and greeters who serve at Sunday morning worship. Do these servants report to the worship pastor or the assimilation pastor? These and other simple misunderstandings are quite commonly at the root of staff difficulties.

The best way to overcome such misunderstandings in roles and titles is to develop written ministry descriptions for each ministry position. Ministry descriptions guard team members from diversified role expectations in the congregation; clarify relationships between ministry jobs;

help avoid overlaps and gaps between positions; provide a foundation for job appraisal; spell out duties, responsibilities, and limits of authority; provide the basis for team evaluation; and build status, respect, and motivation for each team member.

All ministry descriptions should include the following basic ingredients: a statement of title and position, the person to whom the staff member reports, the people who report to the staff member, a statement of duties or areas of responsibility, and a schedule of work time. Staff teams have found that the following guidelines are helpful in developing ministry descriptions.[3] *First,* never ask the team to write an individual's ministry description. Such descriptions normally focus on duties while ignoring objectives. *Second,* let each team member write his or her own ministry description. Each ministry description must be personally tailored to the individual involved and reflect her passion and gifts.

Third, have each team member meet with the senior pastor, or other team leader, to review, revise, and rewrite a final ministry description. *Fourth,* keep the ministry description up-to-date. While a yearly review is obviously needed, it may be wise to have a three-month review so that needed changes can be initiated early in the process after a team member has had time to work under the parameters of the new description.

Fifth, look on the ministry description as a tool to give direction to a team member rather than a formal document to be obeyed. Team members should be free to meet with the team leader as necessary to review or revise their ministry descriptions as their roles change dynamically.

Sixth, share a summary of the various ministry descriptions with the entire congregation. People in the congregation have their own expectations of each member of the team and it is helpful if they are made aware of the prescribed roles and responsibilities of each staff member.

Inequity in Compensation

One of the most difficult problems of team ministry is inequity in salary packages, benefits, or perks among staff members. Some churches do an excellent job of keeping salaries and benefits equitable, but other churches allow for huge differences, which many times lead to ill feelings and poor cooperation among team members. Financial rewards among staff members do not always reflect hours or energy spent. Assistant staff members may put in many more hours than senior staff members who receive a healthier salary. Society teaches us that value is measured by income and even the Bible tells us that a laborer is worthy of his hire. Inequities are a root of many staff problems and need to be addressed.

Inequities in salary can be addressed in several ways. *First,* each staff member needs to rest in the understanding that his ultimate value comes from the Creator and not from the pay package. This will not solve all of the practical problems but is a necessary foundation to any positive staff relationship. *Second,* those responsible for determining staff pay packages must commit themselves to establishing equitable pay for all staff members. As a general rule, the pay scales for a given staff position should be within 15 to 20 percent of the position directly above. For instance, if a senior pastor's pay is more than 15 to 20 percent higher than an associate pastor on the pay scale, the associate team member is likely to feel that inequity exists. Or if the associate pastor's pay is more than 15 to 20 percent above the assistant pastor's, the assistant pastor will feel that inequity exists, and so on down the various positions. *Third,* each staff member must take responsibility as a steward to inform the church leadership of his financial situation. Most pastors find it difficult to talk to church leaders about personal money issues; however, experience has shown that the initiative for providing sound financial information most often begins with the staff member.

Relational Problems

Joining a staff team is like marrying into a family. We do not choose to marry someone based on his or her family. But once we marry, our relationship to our spouse's larger family is important. In the same way, once you join the pastoral staff of a church, all the relationships connected to the staff team become important ingredients to your ministry.

Church staffs are also like families in that certain personalities sometimes do not click. At times it is difficult to get along with or even love members of the family. Habits, lifestyle decisions, or beliefs may create conflict. A few of the key relational problems staffs often encounter follow.

Lack of Trust

Trust levels between staff members are significant because even though team members plan together, they work separately. If the pastoral staff members do not trust each other to carry their own ministry loads, to complete their roles in the grand scheme of things, or to support each other, the team can fail to function. When staff meetings become times for chronic complaining, it is a sign of trouble. Complaints may be simple, such as the office is always too cold or too hot, or more serious, such as they have too much work to do. Moodiness also is a common occurrence and members may feel like they are walking on eggshells never knowing when they will make a comment that will set another staff member off.

Church consultant Dr. William Easum suggests six levels for encouraging trust among teams.[4]

Level One: Staff members are passionate about the vision and direction in which the church is going. *Note:* This level is more caught than taught. Team members either believe in the model or they do not.

Level Two: Team members understand their roles. *Note:* Team members must be able to coach others to do the work of ministry rather than doing the work themselves. This is a major transition for many staff members.

Level Three: Team members are committed to making the necessary changes to team ministry. *Note:* Team ministry functions in an atmosphere of semiconstant change. While some staff members may be able to handle some change, others may not feel comfortable living with it all the time.

Level Four: Team members have a structured way to foster trust. *Note:* There must be built-in systems for communication, such as e-mail, Web pages, retreats, weekly Bible study, sharing, and an assortment of other team-building events.

Level Five: Team members must meet in a small group. *Note:* Teams need to be small enough to get to know each other's hopes and dreams and to become supportive of each other.

Level Six: Team members have an affinity for each other. *Note:* The teams must be made up of people who have a common mission and like each other. It only takes one antagonist to derail the team.

As can be seen, level one focuses only on the external vision to create trust, but level six focuses on internal affinity to develop trust. Moving from level one to level six gradually builds internal trust among team members.

Territorial Attitudes

Territorial issues are likely present when a staff member sees equipment, facilities, or personnel as belonging only to herself. For example, an administrative assistant who is always present whenever a new piece of equipment is delivered to the church office, is the only person allowed to do routine maintenance on the equipment and posts a sign above the equipment announcing that she is the only person able to use it is evidencing a territorial attitude. Another common territorial attitude is seen in a staff member who believes a certain room in the church is her private classroom. If the room has to be used multiple times, the staff member may get visibly upset if she finds coffee cups sitting around or missing pens or pencils.

Team leaders must communicate on a regular basis that the ministry is the Lord's and does not belong to any one individual—including the senior pastor. Therefore, it is expected that each team member will graciously work with all aspects of the ministry in a mutual manner, recognizing that as the church grows, multiple use of facilities and equipment is a necessity.

Unhappy Spouses or Families

It is difficult for a staff member to function successfully when his spouse or family members are unhappy. Such unhappiness can surface regarding a number of issues. For example, feelings of competition may surface if one staff member's area of ministry is growing faster than another's or when someone criticizes a husband's ministry. The natural tendency is to try showing everyone how gifted and committed one's spouse actually is by pointing out other staff members' weaknesses.

Financial inequities may lead to unhappy feelings when it appears one staff member is overpaid. Unhappiness can be the result of a competitive spirit or based on actual inequities. But whatever the cause, a spouse can have enormous impact on the effectiveness of a pastoral staff team. One pastor's wife puts the potential impact this way: "A divided staff can muzzle a church's vitality. A wife's attitude about other staff members has potential to wreck or to promote healthy, harmonious workings among a group of people committed to a common cause."[5]

Managing unhappy families of staff members is extremely difficult. In some cases it may be wise to stay out of the situation and allow the staff member to handle the problem. However, if the unhappiness begins to creep into the staff relationships, destroying harmony and the team's ability to minister effectively, something must be done. The best approach is to seek a win/win between the church and the team member's family by collaborating to discover the problem areas and searching for a workable solution—more on this in the next section.

◢ Resolving Staff Conflict

One of the most frustrating, exasperating, and demanding aspects of leadership is resolving staff conflict. Whenever individuals serve together on a staff team, there is sure to be conflict in at least one of the four main areas noted above. But like Mike in the opening conversation of this chapter, leaders do not always know exactly what to do in a given situation. Thus it is a wise team leader who prepares for conflict. Here are some steps to consider.

First, allow for healthy conflict. It is a mistake to create an atmosphere where conflict is not allowed. By doing so, conflict will still be there but will be stuffed away deep inside the storehouse of feelings in each staff member where it will later explode at an unexpected moment. It is far better to allow for conflict to be expressed a little at a time as it takes place so it can be dealt with gradually. I remember working in a lumberyard just after graduating from high school. Working daily with the raw wood, I often had quite a few small splinters in my hands. The splinters were a mild irritation, which I was able to take care of by removing them as I went along during the day. One day, while working with a hammer and nails, I inadvertently struck my thumb with the hammer. All work stopped as I dropped the hammer and grasped my thumb in pain. When we allow conflicts within our staffs to be addressed as they occur, it is similar to plucking small splinters out of a hand. The work can continue forward when small irritations are dealt with immediately. However, if we force people to stuff their problems, allowing them to build up into huge problems, they will one day come out in greater force and all ministry will stop while the conflict is managed, much like work stopped when I struck my thumb.

Joseph Umidi, professor of ministry at Regent University in Virginia Beach, Virginia, believes that healthy conflict interactions are encouraged as leaders allow for three *P*s: permission, protection, and potency. Permission is given for healthy conflict to take place in the normal process of ministry together. Protection is given to each team member by establishing boundaries so that conflict is managed with respect, appropriate language, and integrity. This allows all staff members to potently express their points of view.[6]

Second, deal with conflict as early as possible. Dr. Norman Shawchuck suggests that conflict moves through five stages.[7]

Stage One: Tension Awareness. Team members begin to sense the breakdown of relationships.

Stage Two: Role Confusion. Team members begin to place blame on others.

Stage Three: Injustice Collecting. Team members begin compiling evidence to justify their position.

Stage Four: Attack Stage. Team members begin to openly express hostility toward other team members.

Stage Five: Adjustment Stage. Team members begin to leave for other ministries or church splits occur.

The key to managing conflict is to deal with it at the earliest stage possible, recognizing that the longer one waits, the more difficult it will be to come to any form of resolution.

Third, practice healthy communication. Conflicts normally create an atmosphere where it is difficult to communicate. However, by following several guidelines, it can be done. It generally is suggested that to communicate in a healthy manner, one must focus on the issue or act rather than on the person, avoid generalities and exaggeration, spell out specific remedies, choose the right time to talk, and follow up to keep communication open.

Fourth, select the proper approach. One of the biggest mistakes in managing conflict is when the leader of the team thinks he must resolve all the issues between staff members. It is natural for staff members to view the senior pastor or other team leader as the Big Daddy or Big Momma who can take care of any and all problems. However, if the leader is a benign, "I'll-take-care-of-your-problem" parent figure, he may be harming the team rather than helping. While this is one approach to managing conflict, there are at least five other approaches that should be considered:

- The Win/Win Option. All parties collaborate to arrive at a meaningful resolution. *Key question:* How can we work together? This approach to managing conflict is the healthiest one and should be used in as many situations as possible. This is sometimes called collaboration.
- The Win/Lose Option. One party seeks to win the conflict at all costs. *Key question:* Is it worth the cost? This approach is best used when core moral, ethical, or biblical values are at stake. This is sometimes called competition.
- The Lose/Yield Option. One party yields to the other after realizing the issue is not worth the trouble. *Key question:* Is it really that important? This approach is best when the conflict focuses on surface or cosmetic issues. This is sometimes called accommodation.

- The Lose/Lose Option. The issue is dropped because it will hurt the church to pursue it to resolution. *Key question:* Will it hurt the church body? This approach is best when core values are not at stake and the issue can be tabled until a later time. This is sometimes called abandonment.
- The Compromise Option. The conflict is ignored allowing the various parties to work out the issues on their own. *Key question:* Is it worth getting involved? This approach is best when it is wisest not to get involved with problems that are beyond your influence. This is sometimes called avoidance.

Dealing with Improper Behavior

As noted in a previous chapter, loyalty to the senior pastor, as well as to the entire pastoral staff team, is a key ingredient for healthy staff relationships. However, loyalty should end when a team member does something immoral, illegal, or dangerous to the staff and church. From a practical perspective, if you find yourself in such a situation, you should take steps to counteract the team member's behavior and, if needed, remove yourself from her area of ministry and authority.

First, document the case as meticulously as possible. Keep running records of meetings, notes, and materials and make copies of all documents. Try to assemble tangible proof of the team member's improper activity. When you think you have the facts, meet with the team member to share your concerns and give him a chance to explain. It may be that your viewpoint is unjustified and meeting with the team member will answer your concerns.

Second, if the issue is not resolved to your satisfaction, place as much distance between yourself and the wrong action as possible for your own protection. While it may not seem fair, it is possible, maybe even probable, that a team member's unwise action will tarnish you as well.

Third, if you have the documentation, it is time to open up the situation as much as possible by getting others involved. Always follow proper lines of authority by going to the person or board directly responsible for the team member you are concerned about. Faulty actions are much more likely to be discovered when several people are involved with the issue.

Fourth, focus on the activity rather than the person involved. The more the issue is depersonalized, the stronger the case will be. If you lose, or discover you were wrong, you will have kept the relationship as strong as possible.

Last, if the offending person is the senior pastor, it is usually best not to go for a win/lose option. Deliberately trying to "fire" your boss usually results in your having to leave the church. If you make it a case of "it's either him or me," it will usually be you. And even if you are successful and the senior pastor leaves, you will probably be branded as the instigator who pushed the pastor out. The next senior pastor will soon learn of your reputation and the working relationship will not be fruitful. Therefore, it is normally in your best interest to move on to another ministry rather than doing all-out battle with the senior pastor. *Remember: When the option is win or lose, you must count the cost of winning and of losing.*

Forbearance

If you have ever watched a hockey game, you have no doubt observed that referees allow the players to fight. The referees only step in to separate players after the players are tired. If hockey referees ventured into the fistfighting too early, not only would they stop the excitement, they would most likely receive some blows themselves. Such forbearance makes sense not only for hockey referees but for team leaders also. As in hockey, too quick an intervention can be counterproductive. Before you enter a conflictive situation between staff members, stop and ask the following questions.

- Would it be beneficial for me to hold back? It may be possible to stop an argument but it could be better to allow all parties to air their grievances.
- Can I learn more by becoming involved than I might otherwise learn? Conflicts occasionally bring out issues of which the leader was not aware. By stepping in too early to manage the conflict, you may lose out on important information.
- Can those involved straighten it out without me? By getting involved too soon, you effectively take away the initiative and potential development of the staff members. If they can work it out themselves, let them.
- Will I be in the middle of the conflict? We know what happens when policemen get in the middle of a family feud. It is wise to proceed with caution rather than jumping into the middle of a staff conflict.

Those ministering on a multiple staff face unique challenges and struggles, one of which is facing conflict. On the whole, conflict is to be avoided. But conflict is an aspect of human nature that is sure to come out in any team situation. Conflictive situations are opportunities for growth and development. The key is for all staff members to accept their roles and to develop a realistic and positive attitude about the circumstances in which they serve, always recognizing for sure that Christ builds his church, not us.

CHAPTER ELEVEN

Leading an Elite Team

There are three keys to making a successful team: (1) Coming together is the beginning. (2) Working together is progress. (3) Staying together is success.

Henry Ford

"How is your staff organized?" inquired Sue Williams of two other associate pastors, as the three were eating lunch together following the monthly pastors' fellowship. "This is my first experience serving on a multiple staff and my senior pastor acts like he's a king. He calls all the shots, dreams up the ideas, determines the goals, generates the enthusiasm, and runs the show. The rest of us do what he tells us to do and report back. There's no question he's the boss. I must admit, however, that things are going well. The tight chain of command structure and the dynamic leadership of the pastor work very effectively. I actually enjoy my work. The only frustrating thing is that the congregation hardly knows any of the rest of the staff is alive. When I first took this posi-

171

tion, I was excited to finally be in an associate position, but most of the people in the congregation look at me like I'm just the senior pastor's assistant. Sometimes I don't even think the congregation knows I'm a pastor."

"I know what you mean," replied Phyl Adamson, who was in her second position as an associate pastor on a large pastoral staff team. "My first experience on a multiple staff was similar to yours but now I'm serving on a team that is the other extreme. My senior pastor exerts little or no influence in giving direction to the staff. He actually abdicates his role as leader, which leaves our staff team feeling like we're adrift at sea with no sense of direction. Staff meetings are rarely held, the senior pastor is always too busy to meet with me, and he's usually unavailable to the rest of the staff also. Our staff team has almost no sense of cohesiveness. We operate in a do-it-your-own-way atmosphere of trial and error. To be perfectly frank, I'm extremely discouraged."

"Listening to you two makes me grateful for the team I'm on," Tom Watson, the third member of the group, said. "The staff I serve on operates more like a team. I am an equal partner colaboring together in the gospel with the rest of the staff. The senior pastor oversees and supervises each of us as a 'first' among equals. I've never seen him acting superior, but functionally he is ultimately responsible for the overall direction of the church and staff. I minister within a clearly defined job description that matches my passions and gifts. What I enjoy the most is that the senior pastor gives me a lot of freedom to develop my particular area of ministry. Of course, he does work closely with me, offering suggestions, acting as a sounding board, and holding me to my goals."

This conversation illustrates three common approaches to team leadership. Sue Williams serves on a staff with the approach of "senior pastor is king." Sometimes this approach is called the ship analogy. The captain of the ship represents the senior pastor who determines the priorities, directs the expenditure of resources, and commands the direction.

Associate and assistant pastors serve as helmsmen, steering and coordinating individual areas of responsibility so that the ship reaches its destination.[1]

Phyl Adamson serves on a staff that uses the "leaderless staff" approach. This approach operates on the assumption that each staff member is an expert in her field and should know what to do with little or no direction from the senior pastor. This type of team is often described as a star. Each point of the star represents a ministry area served by a professional in that area. All full-time paid pastors serve toward a common ministry, with each one representing a distinct and equal point of the star. Such an approach to team ministry may function well for a time, but the staff members usually end up working at odds with each other, with differing visions, goals, and purpose. Eventually the church grinds to a halt due to the lack of common direction at the staff team level.

Tom Watson serves on a staff that uses the "collaborative team" approach. This type of team can be described as a van. When several people ride together in a van, they all can give advice, plan, and work together to determine the direction the van goes. Of course, only one person can drive at a time. A church staff is on a journey and everyone can offer advice, help plan, and formulate direction. However, only one person can drive, usually the senior pastor. At times other staff members may take over the wheel, depending on the needs of the moment and the giftedness of the staff members. In most situations, however, the driver is the senior pastor and he has the responsibility of guiding and pacing the staff so they arrive safely at their destination.

Naturally there are numerous hybrids of team ministry. One example is that of a sports team. In this approach the senior pastor is either the coach or the quarterback. In either case, it is the senior pastor's responsibility to "call the plays." The rest of the staff are trained and disciplined toward the fulfillment of a particular game plan most often predetermined by the senior pastor and certain lay leaders. Loyalty to the team is most important for such a team to function effectively. This style of team is a hybrid of the collaborative team and the pastor is king approaches.

◣ Shifting to Collaborative Teams

As we enter the twenty-first century, one of the mega-changes in both profit and nonprofit sectors of our society is the shift from centralized to decentralized structures. The impact of this shift is being felt in all organizations such as credit unions, major corporations, denominational hierarchies, and local churches. A general comparison of the two approaches looks like the following:

Centralization	Decentralization
Provides control	Enables trust
Establishes power	Encourages understanding
Stresses organizational needs	Focuses on customer needs
Offers consistency of process	Allows for faster decisions
Operates on systems	Provides greater flexibility
Consolidates authority at the top	Enables local authority
Motivates through coercion	Motivates through influences
Creates fortress mentality	Creates missional mentality

A centralized structure works best when the concern is to create economies of scale to reduce costs or when attempting to derive the maximum impact from investments. For example, few local churches send out their own missionaries to foreign countries. Most have found that by using a centralized organization (mission agency), more missionaries can be deployed at a reduced cost.

Decentralized structures work best when the concern is to provide resources that are tailored to individual needs or when attempting to provide a quicker response to complex challenges. For example, most local churches create unique programming to address the felt needs in their particular communities. As the needs change, the programming can change quickly to speak to emerging issues.

For the most part, the changing, complex environment in which churches find themselves in the twenty-first century means that centralized, oppressive, top-down approaches to ministry are being replaced by decentralized, life-giving, bottom-up approaches.

At the heart of this shift to decentralization is collaborative team ministry. According to church consultant Dan Reeves, such teams have the following characteristics.[2]

- The vision is grassroots initiated and owned.
- The staff members function as coaches developing lay teams.
- Team members are connected by a compelling owned vision.
- The teams are fluid and focused on a task.
- Team members have a deep-seated belief in the power and synergy of teams.
- Team members experience a climate of trust.
- Team members practice open and honest communication.
- Conflict is viewed as a normal means of creatively exploring new ideas.

Characteristics like these mature fastest in a collaborative climate. Recent research by Drs. Carl Larson and Frank LaFasto define such a climate this way: "Collaborative climate refers to the extent to which members communicate openly, disclose problems, share information, help each other overcome obstacles, and discover ways of succeeding."[3] By all current measures, it appears that effective pastoral staff teams of the twenty-first century will reflect more of a collaborative approach than a pastor is king or leader-less team approach.

◢◣ A Caution

A Leader Is Needed

The idea of collaborative team ministry is clearly a biblical concept with roots in the Old Testament example of the Godhead and the New Testament example of Jesus training the twelve disciples. Unfortunately one of the dangers in the shift to collaborative team ministry is a belief that teams can be leaderless. Phyl Adamson's description of a "leaderless team" is not what is meant by collaborative team ministry.

It must not be forgotten that as God the Father is the head of the Godhead and Jesus was the head of the disciples, so there must be a leader of any team. Martin Anderson addressed this same issue in his 1965 book *Multiple Ministries:*

> A multiple ministry is a team operation, but a team must have a leader. In nature two heads is freakish, and it is not good in the church. Whether in business, school, government or the church, there must be one head. Order is a fundamental necessity. This requires that someone be in charge. There must be a place of ultimate responsibility. There are so many situations in which someone must make the final decision.[4]

In retrospect, the use of the term *head* is probably not the best term since Paul clearly states that Christ is the head of the church (Eph. 1:22; 5:23). Obviously Anderson's use of the term *head* does not imply that the earthly leader of a team takes the place of Christ, which is impossible, but only that every team needs a point person. Jerry Brown, in *Church Staff Teams That Win,* argues, "The team has to have a recognized quarterback or captain."[5]

The most important ingredient in collaborative team performance is the presence of an effective team leader. Gen. Dwight D. Eisenhower made the following observation from his experiences in World War II:

> I have developed almost an obsession as to the certainty with which you can judge a division, or any other large unit, merely by knowing its commander intimately. Of course, we have had pounded into us all through our school courses that the exact level of a commander's personality and ability is always reflected in his unit—but I did not realize, until opportunity came for comparisons on a rather large scale, how infallibly the commander and unit are almost one and the same thing.[6]

The bottom line is someone must be charged with decision making and, as we discussed in chapter 5, the senior pastor is the logical person in the great majority of cases. For the senior pastor to act as supervisor of the staff team implies that

1. He has discretionary veto power.
2. The buck stops with him.
3. He makes the decisions in "go, no go" situations.
4. He is aware of the entire picture of the church.
5. He gives moral, spiritual, managerial, and personal support to the staff.

The Leader as Model

It is clear that a pastoral staff team will take on the characteristics and personality of a long-term pastor. This occurs quite naturally over a five-to-seven–year period of time, as the pastor's leadership style and personality attract similar people to the ministry. This is a sobering realization for most pastors, but one that should not be rejected. As Paul invited his followers to imitate his walk and follow his example (1 Cor. 4:16; 11:1; Phil. 3:17), so should a senior pastor expect others to follow his model.

What are the special qualities that a leader needs to model in leadership in the twenty-first century? Here are a few that most people agree on:

- Perception of Reality. Team leaders need a grasp of what is really taking place around them. They must live in the present and future not just the past. Leaders see what is really going on.
- Team-Building Skill. Team leaders need a positive regard for collaborative ministry, the courage to let go of control, and an ability to communicate.
- Decisive Temperament. Team leaders need to have a balanced ability to make less important decisions quickly and not to make more important decisions prematurely.
- Tenacity. Team leaders need a spirit that absorbs disappointments and keeps moving forward.
- Integrity. Team leaders need a quality of life that engenders trust from fellow team members. The foundation of leadership is character rather than charisma.
- Coaching Ability. Team leaders need to be the spiritual coaches, creating a healthy environment for the team members.

The number one assignment of leaders in the twenty-first century is to develop other leaders. Nonleaders are interested in self-development, but leaders are interested in developing others.

Being a strong leader while being a servant is a key aspect of the leadership that Jesus modeled. Throughout his entire earthly ministry, Jesus demonstrated strength, combined with humility, while constantly refusing to be overbearing with people. Senior pastors and other team leaders must lead multiple staff teams with the same heart.

◤ Stages of Team Development

Students of team development have recognized that teams go through various stages of development. One of the most popular characterizations of that development is forming, storming, norming, and performing. At each stage the team leader has a different role to play.

Forming

When a team first comes together, everyone is trying to figure out how they fit with each other. What are the team goals? How do roles, tasks, and responsibilities play out? How much authority does one have to make decisions? Who reports to whom?

At this stage the team leader needs to adopt a directing style of leadership by providing specific instructions and closely supervising the staff team. The leader will most often be the senior pastor, although there are a few situations where an executive staff member may fill this role. Since leadership abhors a vacuum, if there is no designated leader some person will rise to the surface to take charge. It may be as simple as calling the meeting to order, assigning work, or calling team members to account, but someone will take the lead.

Teams do not just happen; they have to be built. It is up to the team leader to assist in forming the team into a cohesive group during this developmental stage. Team members need time and opportunities to get to know each other in informal, comfortable environments. Thus the leader must provide the time and opportunities for the team to grow together.

Most important, however, is a clear purpose or vision around which the team can rally.

A demanding performance challenge tends to create a team. The hunger for performance is far more important to team success than team-building exercises, special incentives, or team leaders with ideal profiles. In fact, teams often form around such challenges without any help or support from management. Conversely, potential teams without such challenges usually fail to become teams.[7]

The team leader must help the team develop a compelling vision for their future ministry. If the team can face a particular challenge or goal together, it will help bond them into a team.

Storming

As team members begin to work together, problems will crop up. During this stormy stage, team members may challenge and question the team leader. Some call this the "shoot-the-leader stage" due to the many questions that come up, such as, Is our purpose the right one? Are we on the right track? Are we making progress?

The leader's job during this stage is to persuade and assure the team members. Thus the team leader will find that a coaching style of leadership is helpful during this period of the team's development. Popular author Stephen Covey suggests:

> Dependent people need others to get what they want. Independent people can get what they want through their own effort. Interdependent people combine their own efforts with the efforts of others to achieve their greatest success.[8]

To build an interdependent team during this stormy period, members need a lot of emotional, spiritual, and personal support. Leaders must be comfortable with some conflict and challenges and their listening and coaching skills are particularly crucial at this time.

Norming

Team members will eventually arrive at a set of written or unwritten rules as to how they will interact with each other. A team covenant will be agreed on and values will be established to guide the team. When norms are reached, the team leader must adopt a supporting style of leadership, allowing the norms to guide the team in a powerful, unspoken manner. Decision making in the norming stage is by consensus. "Consensus decisions take time and patience, but the decisions that result from a consensus are usually superior to decisions made by the brightest member of the group."[9] However, consensus leadership should not be construed as being without disagreement. Divergent opinions ought to be accepted and even expected. Peter Drucker suggests:

> All the first-rate decision-makers I've observed, beginning with Franklin D. Roosevelt, had a very simple rule: If you have consensus on an important matter, don't make the decision. Adjourn it so that everybody has a little time to think. Important decisions are risky. They should be controversial. Acclamation means that nobody has done the homework.[10]

Performing

The team begins to fulfill their tasks by producing the work for which they have been added to the staff team. A team leader can settle into more of a delegating style of leadership during this phase, which will allow him more time for analyzing and planning for the future. By delegating, the leader turns over responsibility and authority for decision making and problem solving to the staff members.

However, a team leader must contribute to the team with real work.

Everyone on a real team, including the leader, does real work in roughly equivalent amounts. Team leaders do have a certain distance from the team by virtue of their position, but they do not use that distance "just to sit back and make decisions." Team leaders must contribute in whatever way the team needs, just like any other member. Moreover, team leaders do not delegate the nasty jobs to others. Where personal risks are high or "dirty work" is required, the team leader should step forward.[11]

▗▖ The Team Playbook

In seven seasons from 1983 to 1989 the football team of Augustana College in Rock Island, Illinois, built a record of 77-5-1 and won four NCAA Division III championships. The offensive playbook they used during those years was so small it could be diagrammed on a napkin. It contained only six running plays and four passing plays. It was not the size of their playbook or the number of plays that led to such a great record. Rival coaches agreed: "Augustana knows that you know what they've got. But their execution is terrific."[12]

Elite teams know how to execute their game plan. All effective team leaders learn how to focus their staff's energy, leverage their efforts, and align their work to achieve superior results. How do they do this? By working with the following fundamental guidelines.

Build a Movement

Leaders in the twenty-first century are not simply managers of church programs. They are leaders of movements that help people on spiritual journeys find spiritual meaning. Church staffs must feel they are part of a spiritual movement that is memorable. This means defining a meaningful vision for the future.

182

Nothing happens until someone defines a vision. There was no NASA space program until John F. Kennedy proclaimed his vision to "put a man on the moon by the end of the decade." McDonald's was a single restaurant until Ray Kroc assumed leadership with a vision for restaurants throughout the United States and the world. One of the most critical roles a leader plays is to define the direction for the church and staff. Clyde McDowell says:

> Just as you do, every staff member faces staggering people demands, administrative duties, and hurried deadlines. As you help your staff members maintain their focus on the essentials, you equip them to overcome their guilt and feeling of "I'm not getting my job done." Remember that the unrelenting pace of ministry often tends to keep ministry professionals "bogged down" in the current crisis. As you focus on defining and communicating your mission, you can help your staff members see beyond the "bog" and give hope for the next phase of the task.[13]

Elite teams are drawn together by a clearly defined mission for which all the team members have a passion. It is next to impossible to have an effective team when everyone is heading in a different direction. Thus the senior pastor must keep the purpose, vision, and goals relevant and meaningful to the staff members.

Share the Leadership

In the complex ministry climate of the twenty-first century, effective leaders understand that they do not have all the wisdom, knowledge, or tools to be successful. They must build a team that is willing to share leadership among the team, based on the team's needs and the skill sets of each individual member. Thus a senior pastor will give way for other team members to take the lead when their skills are obviously the ones most applicable to the situation.

At times a senior pastor will need to be directive, but more often he will need to use participative management of the team. All team members have a unique contribution to make to the overall success of the team and they need the opportunity to voice their viewpoints. This should not lead to the conclusion that every team member has an equal vote on every issue, as Thomas Quick confirms in his book *Successful Team Building:*

> This does not necessarily mean that all organizations practicing participative management are democratic. Not everyone has an equal vote. It's possible that not all decisions are voted on. What is likely is that everyone has the privilege of trying to influence the decision-making process when the decision affects him or her. At the very least, employees in a participative environment are confident that management does not knowingly and arbitrarily make decisions that are contrary to the welfare of employees.[14]

Leaders of twenty-first–century churches know that the more controls they place on team members, the less likely they will excel. Thus leaders do not seek to control as much as they equip staff members to act.

Empower Decision Making

Good leaders are problem givers more than problem solvers. They believe that problems should be passed down the line to people as close to the action as possible. Decisions arrived at by the decision makers who are close to the action will always, over time, be better than those dictated from the top down, no matter how brilliant the leader may be.

Most team leaders oversee staff members who know more about many aspects of their ministries than the senior pastor does. Therefore, when decisions are to be made that affect team members, the senior pastor should not hesitate to ask team members for their input. And he needs to listen. The team leader should offer his own ideas only after having heard and understood the views of the team. This makes the team members more receptive to the final outcomes of decisions and helps ensure that ideas are not out in left field. George Bullard, a church consultant, states:

> Pastors, staff ministers, and key church leaders may best express leadership through projecting importance, shared goals, and clear values. Then they need to get out of the way and allow the people they have recruited to do the work, to actually do the work.[15]

Consultant William Easum echoes this and suggests three steps for empowering teams. *First,* share all information. *Second,* create autonomy through boundaries such as mission, vision, values, and belief statements. *Third,* replace as much of the hierarchy as possible with teams throughout the church.[16]

Multiply Leaders

The job description of every staff person should be to grow future leaders. Dale E. Galloway, former pastor of New Hope Community Church in Portland, Oregon, says that the most important lesson he learned is "All staff members must multiply themselves through lay leader development." Each staff member's job description should begin the same way, "It's your primary responsibility to recruit, motivate, and train lay people for ministry and to build small groups or teams."[17] Leaders of elite teams make certain all the staff members who are hired understand they are to focus on lay leader development.

Encourage Growth

The moment the team stops learning, it stops leading. Team leaders are always on the lookout for ways to improve the team's skills. "If the ax is dull and its edge unsharpened, more strength is needed but skill will bring success" (Eccles. 10:10). Senior pastors who lead elite teams encourage growth, give away ownership, and show support to the team by providing opportunities for growth and development.

To increase the creativity of team members, leaders of elite teams ask the members to fail at least twice a year. Yes! actually fail by attempting several creative new ministries. Not only does this encourage growth, but 70 percent of the new ministries will take hold, increasing the overall ministry of the church. To get the staff members to do this, however, the team leader cannot shoot those who do fail.

Assess Team Performance

Evaluation always precedes growth and improvement. The question must be asked and answered, How well is the team doing? Elite teams assess themselves on a regular timetable. As a rule, teams are harder on themselves than individuals are because they will share responsibility.

> At its core, Team accountability is about the sincere promises we make to ourselves and others, promises that underpin two critical aspects of teams: commitment and trust. By promising to hold ourselves accountable to the team's goals, we each earn the right to express our own views about all aspects of the team's effort and to have our views receive a fair and constructive hearing. By following through on such a promise, we preserve and extend the trust upon which any team must be built.[18]

Glenn Varney, author of *Building Productive Teams*, writes, "For effective teamwork, the success of the team must supersede individual success: that is, individuals win or lose as a team."[19] Establishing a win/win mentality is less confrontational and moves from using power to sharing it, emphasizing partnering rather than ultimatums.

Coach with Care

The senior pastor has got to be more than a demanding boss to the staff members. When a crisis comes to a staff member's family, they need someone to come to for pastoral care. Leaders of elite teams manage like Jesus.

> Jesus was committed to a caring approach to managing his disciples. He didn't see his disciples as objects to be manipulated for his success, but rather as human beings to be inspired and developed. However, he never let their unethical conduct go unchecked or poor performance unnoticed. He addressed them directly and openly, and always supported and encouraged individual changes of heart.[20]

Dan Reiland, a consultant with Injoy, suggests that a caring coach:

1. demonstrates a personal lifestyle worthy of modeling
2. maintains a consistent pattern of availability
3. is genuinely interested in the person being coached
4. is an excellent listener and discerner of people
5. demonstrates the ability to be patient with people[21]

Have Fun

A happy staff is a motivated staff. Team members enjoy the team when they are allowed to stretch a bit and use a variety of skills, tasks have a visible outcome, work is viewed as important, autonomy is allowed, and feedback is continually given. Beyond these predictable aspects, a team leader can creatively work to make the team a fun group to belong to by occasionally doing unusual, even crazy things, such as taking the team to an amusement park or going to a museum or concert. The event does not matter as long as it is enjoyable and allows the team to relax together.

Remember: Teamwork is a picture of God's design for community. Be sure to give recognition and appreciation.

One of the most popular management approaches of the past decade is called "managing by walking around." The idea is to get out among the people to really discover what is taking place. Playing on this concept of management, an anonymous person jokingly suggested the following "real world" approaches to leadership:

1. *Managing by hiding information.* Information hiders are aware of the market value of secret information. Staff members will be very thankful to get any information at all from these leaders.
2. *Managing by using buzz words.* These leaders attempt to bluff you with hip, nearly undefined terms. They say things like, "It is crucial that you integrate your platform with innovative telecommunication as described on www.network.org."
3. *Managing by reorganization.* If these leaders think there is nothing more to organize, they reorganize. Their task is to keep you busy at all costs.
4. *Managing by conceptual thinking.* These leaders explain the present situation from a theoretical view of the future. The thought that their ideas will never work completely satisfies them because they will always have something to talk about.
5. *Managing BUA (by using abbreviations).* This leadership style is ATRASACWOC (adopted to reach a shorter and clearer way of communication).

Clearly, one does not develop an elite team by using these or many other nonproductive styles of leadership and management. Building an elite team takes careful thought and work. Employing the ideas found throughout this chapter will put you on the right track.

CHAPTER **TWELVE**

Defining the Future

> The most successful leader of all is one who sees another picture not yet actualized.
>
> Mary Parker Follett

"All I know is things have really changed!" Mike Baines and Bill Duggan were talking over coffee. It had become a regular Thursday morning ritual and a time for mutual encouragement and counsel. But Mike's comment was completely out of context and caught Bill by surprise.

"What do you mean, Mike?" he asked.

"I mean pastoring a church and staffing a church! Just in the short time I've been pastoring, everything has changed!"

"For instance . . . ?" Bill was pretty sure that during his forty-three years of pastoring, he had experienced it all. He figured Mike was just feeling overwhelmed—the way Bill used to feel before his retirement last year.

"Well, for starters it seems that churches now expect their staff members to understand the true value of teamwork. The days of the lone ranger pastor are gone. Staff members will have to believe in and practice true collaboration and cooperation to be fruitful in this century."

"That makes sense and seems very biblical," Bill agreed. "What else have you discovered over the last few months?"

"I've found that a good team member expects the church he or she serves to have a clarity of purpose, vision, and values," Mike continued. "A team can't accomplish much if they don't know what the goals are."

"True! True." Bill nodded. "You know, I've heard several pastors talk lately about how they must keep growing to stay up with the changing face of church ministry. Pastoral growth must be one of those values."

"Yes, it is," Mike agreed. "But, there are several other values that are important too. For instance, I've found that staff members want to be treated fairly, especially when it comes to compensation. They desire recognition and honest feedback that focuses more on the positive than the negative."

"You're right, Mike. It sounds like staff members and churches are operating under a different set of expectations than they used to."

"Exactly! It certainly hasn't all been worked out yet," Mike explained, "but what we seem to be coming up with is a new social contract."

"A new social contract?" Bill was confused. "What do you mean?"

"When people are together, there is always a guiding set of principles, rules, and values that define their relationship. Sometimes such guidelines are written down, like when a workers' union enters into a contract with a factory. However, there are unwritten guidelines that are called a social contact. It defines the expectations and relationships between groups of people."

"So that's what you meant when you said everything is changing," Bill interrupted. "You mean that the social contract, or relationship, between churches and staff is changing."

"You've got it," Mike confirmed. "The way I see it, the command-and-control relationships are beating a fast retreat. In their place are teaming, open communication, and flexibility."

Questions concerning church ministry are ultimately social questions—they involve how people work together and interact. While the exact details are still being worked out, the changes in the social contracts as Bill and Mike discussed are being reshaped in these first years of the twenty-first century. The unwritten agreement under which churches, senior pastors, and staff members minister is taking on a different form and dimension. As discussed earlier in this book, it is clear that churches are expecting much more from their staff then previously. Today churches look to hire staff members with a larger portfolio of skills and competencies than was required just a decade ago. Counterbalancing the church's changing expectations, staff members seem to look for increased appreciation and an enriching environment in which to minister. These are just two of the many expectations pastors bring to staff ministry today. This new social contract is still being formulated as churches and staff work out mutually satisfying relationships. When it will be in final form is anyone's guess. However, five broad ideas will likely be major aspects of the unwritten agreement. These broad ideas have to do with direction, learning and innovation, high expectations, technology, and appreciation.

◤ A Clear Direction

Purpose, vision, and values are three buzz words that were often heard in churches during the past decade. However, they are words that can have real substance. Only the churches that have a clear sense of direction will see much growth in the coming decades. It makes sense that effective staff teams must be committed to their church's purpose, vision, and values. To gain such a commitment, however, staff members must have an active part in crating the purpose, vision, and values of the churches they serve. This involves not only the development of the purpose, vision, and values but an understanding of how these elements align with their personal and family purpose, vision, and values.

▚ A Learning Environment

Under the new social contract, staff members will be selected not for what they already know but for how fast they can learn. It is not so important to be able to access information in the twenty-first century, but to be able to differentiate relevant information from the exponentially multiplying masses of nonrelevant information.

This means that constant training will be the norm. Churches that hope to fulfill Christ's mission to reach the lost must provide for ongoing staff training with a variety of programs: sabbaticals, continuing education, seminars.

Additionally, churches must be willing to let staff members innovate and attempt creative new ministries. As the last half of the twentieth century was a time of organization, the first half of the twenty-first century will be a time of innovation. Churches and staff members will excel by demonstrating a high degree of flexibility and adaptability in dealing with people, technology, and the changing ministry environment. In the midst of change they will realize the importance of remaining connected to people. Staff desire an environment where they can take disciplined risks to develop new forms and styles of ministry.

▚ A Challenging Atmosphere

From all appearances, social and spiritual forces will continue to create ongoing change, which will demand more from churches and staff members. Some researchers predict the differences between 1900 and 2000 will be less extreme than the differences between 2000 and 2010. If this comes to pass, church leaders will be faced with rethinking staff competencies and redefining working relationships.

The new social contract requires churches to hold staff members accountable to higher levels of excellence and performance, but to do so churches must provide the necessary resources for success. Among the obvious resources of office, up-to-date equipment, and an above-average budget, there must be a stimulating ministry environment, an understanding of the needs of staff members, and a church to which staff members are proud to be dedicated.

A Connected Relationship

During the past two decades, more than twenty-five million computers have been added to the tools of the general workforce in the United States. Cellular telephone subscriptions jumped from zero in 1983 to sixteen million in one decade. By the mid-1990s nineteen million people carried pagers and close to twelve billion messages were left in pager mailboxes.

The new social contract calls for churches to realize that most professionals in all fields have computers on their desks and telephones in their pockets. Technology allows staff to connect with others almost anywhere and anytime. For church staffs to operate successfully, they must be resourced with up-to-date technology to remain connected to people who are removed from others in space, thought, and emotion.

A Sense of Appreciation

In a rapidly changing world, excellent staff members will be a prime ingredient of church growth. Churches must accommodate the desire of staff members for self-fulfillment. Thus, under the new social contract, staff members must receive appropriate appreciation and recognition. Three core issues that staff members look for are fair compensation, relevant feedback, and recognition for their contribution. To balance these desires, staff members must willingly accept accountability to a high level of performance, effort, and excellence.

The challenge of growing a fruitful church ministry in the next few decades is significant. What may be required above all, however, is a fundamental rethinking of the need for, value of, and approach to team ministry. The changing face of ministry demands interdependent teams, because few individuals will be capable of knowing or doing it all. The main challenge for churches is finding and keeping excellent staff members. This will require a balancing of different interests—the new social contract.

Like most things in life that are worthwhile, implementing the answers to our staffing questions requires determination, practice, and sensitivity to the Holy Spirit. *Staff Your Church for Growth* is a beginning point that will assist you in heading in the right direction. How your church and staff actually meld together for faithful ministry is up to you. As we have seen, there is a variety of approaches. May God richly bless your ministry as you seek to staff your church for growth!

Notes

Chapter 1 *No Longer the Lone Ranger*

1. Bruce W. Jones, *Ministerial Leadership in a Managerial World* (Wheaton: Tyndale House, 1988), 160.

2. Lyle E. Schaller, "Act Your Size!" *Church Management* (March 1988), 42.

3. Edward L. R. Elson, "Memorable Years in a Washington Pulpit," *Christianity Today* (March 30, 1973), 18.

4. Schaller, "Act Your Size!" 42.

5. C. Peter Wagner, *Leading Your Church to Growth* (Ventura, Calif.: Regal, 1984), 212.

Chapter 2 *Staffing for Growth*

1. Carol S. Childress, "The Future Tense Church" (handout distributed at the Church in the 21st Century conference, Minneapolis, Minn., June 28, 1994), 5.

2. Jolene L. Roehlkepartain, "Youth Ministry: Its Impact on Church Growth," *Group* (September 1989), 25.

3. William M. Easum, "Developing a Multiple Staff," *21st Century Strategies Inc.* (1994), 3.

4. Quoted in *Ministry Advantage* 8, no. 1 (winter 1998), 4.

5. Lyle E. Schaller, *The Multiple Staff and the Larger Church* (Nashville: Abingdon Press, 1980), 81.

Chapter 3 *Adding Team Members*

1. Martin Anderson, *Multiple Ministries* (Minneapolis: Augsburg, 1965), 5.

2. Herman J. Sweet, *The Multiple Staff in the Local Church* (Philadelphia: Westminster Press, 1963), 56.

3. Ibid., 57–58.

4. Schaller, *The Multiple Staff and the Larger Church,* 59.

5. Wagner, *Leading Your Church to Growth,* 212.

6. Based on a comparison of ministers to churches as found in the *Yearbook of American and Canadian Churches* from 1915 to the present.

7. Schaller, *The Multiple Staff and the Larger Church,* 83.

8. John C. LaRue Jr., "Church Staffing Levels and Expenses," *Your Church* (November–December 1993), 48.

9. Ibid.

10. For further insights on hiring homegrown staff, see Alan Nelson, "Home-Grown Staff," *Vital Ministry* (January–February 1998), 27–29.

11. Lyle E. Schaller, *The Senior Minister* (Nashville: Abingdon Press, 1988), 174.

Chapter 4 *Recruiting Staff*

1. "What Executive Pastors Are Talking About," *Church Champions Letter* 3 (May–June 1998), 1.

2. Steve Jobs, quoted by Debra Phillips in "Books Section," *Entrepreneur* (June 1997), 236.

3. Pat MacMillan, *Hiring Excellence* (Colorado Springs: NavPress, 1992), 18.

4. Wagner, *Leading Your Church to Growth,* 213–14.

5. Charles D. Olsen, "Building and Leading a Pastoral Team" (D.Min. diss., Talbot School of Theology, May 1996).

6. Peter F. Drucker, *The Effective Executive* (New York: Harper and Row, 1966), 87.

7. Ibid., 32.

8. Herb Miller, "How to Select Additional Staff," *Net Results* XVII, no. 8 (August 1996): 8.

9. Pierre Mornell, "Zero Defect Hiring," *Inc.* (March 1998), 82.

10. Harold J. Westing, *Multiple Church Staff Handbook* (Grand Rapids: Kregel, 1985), 148.

11. Peter F. Drucker, *Managing the Non-Profit Organization* (New York: HarperCollins, 1990), 148.

12. Some of the material used in this chapter was adapted from Glen S. Martin, "Nine Principles for Hiring New Staff Members," in *The McIntosh Church Growth Network* 10, no. 6 (June 1998), 1–2.

Chapter 5 *Appreciating Team Roles*

1. John Vaughan, "What It Takes to Be a Growth Leader," *Growing Churches* (October–December 1993), 55.

2. Charles R. Swindoll, *Leadership* (Waco, Tex.: Word, 1985), 7.

3. Schaller, *The Multiple Staff and the Larger Church,* 108–9.

4. Ibid., 110–11.

5. Ibid., 111–16.

6. Stephen R. Covey, *Principle-Centered Leadership* (New York: Simon and Schuster, 1990), 246.

7. Jerry Rueb, "The Large Church Phenomenon," *B.C. Baptist Fellowship* 45, no. 3 (March 1992), 2.

8. Easum, "Developing a Multiple Staff," 11.

9. Ibid.

10. Marvin T. Judy, *The Multiple Staff Ministry* (Nashville: Abingdon Press, 1969), 30.

Chapter 6 *Teaming Together*

1. Earl Radmacher, "The Jack-of-All-Trades Syndrome," *Moody Monthly* 71, no. 7 (March 1971), 41–43.

2. Schaller, *The Multiple Staff and the Larger Church*, 53.

3. R. Daniel Reeves, "Mega-Shifting to a Team Ministry Approach," *Ministry Advantage* 8, no. 1 (winter 1998), 2.

4. Lou Bainbridge, "Lou Bainbridge Builds Teams," *Fast Company* (December 1998), 228.

5. Reeves, "Mega-Shifting to a Team Approach," 3.

Chapter 7 *Nurturing a Healthy Staff*

1. Warren Bennis and Patricia Ward Biederman, "The Secrets of Creative Collaboration," *Inc.* (December 1996), 99.

2. Anderson, *Multiple Ministries*, 31.

3. Clyde McDowell, "10 Ways to Support Your Staff," *Vital Ministry* (January–February 1998), 38.

4. John Keegan, *The Face of Battle* (New York: Viking Press, 1976), 53.

5. Auren Uris, *The Executive Deskbook* (New York: Van Nostrand Reinhold, 1976), 39.

6. Kenneth R. Mitchell, *Multiple Staff Ministries* (Philadelphia: Westminster Press, 1988), 42.

7. Doran C. McCarty, *Working with People* (Nashville: Broadman Press, 1986), 62.

8. Jon R. Katzenbach and Douglas K. Smith, *The Wisdom of Teams* (New York: HarperCollins, 1993), 21.

9. McCarty, *Working with People*, 61.

10. Quoted in Keegan, *The Face of Battle*, 73.

11. Ronald W. Wiebe and Bruce A. Rowlison, *Let's Talk about Church Staff Relationships* (Alhambra, Calif.: Green Leaf, 1983), 46.

12. Melvin Edmundson, "Building Staff Relationships," *Journal of Church Music* 28, no. 3 (March 1986): 13–14.

13. George Bullard, *Champions Book Notes* 1, no. 10 (May 1998), 1.

14. McDowell, "10 Ways to Support Your Staff," 40.

15. Drucker, *Managing the Non-Profit Organization*, 18–19.

16. Quoted by Steven W. Brown, *13 Fatal Errors Managers Make and How You Can Avoid Them* (New York: Berkeley Books, 1985), 56.

17. Adapted from McCarty, *Working with People*, 75.

18. Michael Woodruff, "Managing Your Ministry," *Youthworker* XI, no. 1 (summer 1994), 81.

19. Jerry Brown, *Church Staff Teams That Win* (Nashville: Convention Press, 1979), 85.

Chapter 8 *Motivating a Superior Staff*

1. Reeves, "Mega-Shifting to a Team Ministry Approach," 1.

2. Rick Warren, "Building a Team Spirit in Your Staff," *Ministry Advantage* 8, no. 1 (winter 1998), 6.

3. Brown, *Church Staff Teams That Win*, 85.

4. Kenneth Blanchard and Spencer Johnson, *The One Minute Manager* (New York: William Morrow, 1981), 44.

5. David Andersen, "He Was My Mentor," *The American Baptist* (September 1982), 12.

6. Ted W. Engstrom and Edward R. Dayton, *The Art of Management for Christian Leaders* (Waco: Word, 1976), 163.

7. Drucker, *Managing the Non-Profit Organization*, 18–19.

8. Thomas Peters and Robert Waterman Jr., *In Search of Excellence* (New York: Harper and Row, 1982).

9. Philip M. Van Auken, "Leading in Four Arenas," *Management World* (winter 1992), 14–16.

10. John C. Maxwell, *Developing the Leader within You* (Nashville: Thomas Nelson, 1993), 168.

11. Robert J. Kriegel and Louis Patler, *If It Ain't Broke, Break It!* (New York: Warner Books, 1991), 259.

Chapter 9 *Discipling Up*

1. Quoted by Michael Woodruff in "Managing Your Ministry," 77.

2. Ibid.

3. Engstrom and Dayton, *The Art of Management for Christian Leaders*, 2.

4. Ted Engstrom and Ed Dayton, "Making Your Boss Successful," *Christian Leadership Letter* (October 1987), 1.

Chapter 10 *Managing Staff Conflicts*

1. Harold J. Westing, talk presented at a pastors' symposium seminar, Talbot School of Theology, La Mirada, Calif., October 12–13, 1987.

2. Quoted by Jessica Guynn in "Bullies in the Workplace," *The San Diego Union Tribune*, December 28, 1998, p. C-1.

3. Adapted from Harold J. Westing, "Describing Your Mission," in *Church Staff Handbook* (Grand Rapids: Kregel, 1997), 94–95.

4. William Easum, "Teams," at www.easum.com, September 22, 1998, 3.

5. Marilyn Hansen, "When Your Husband Is Part of a Staff," *Partnership* (March–April 1985), 49.

6. Joseph Umidi, "How to Resolve Conflict among Your Church Staff," *Ministries Today* (January–February 1998), 36.

7. Cited in Umidi, "How to Resolve Conflict among Your Church Staff."

Chapter 11 *Leading an Elite Team*

1. Westing, *Church Staff Handbook,* 42–43.

2. Reeves, "Mega-Shifting to a Team Ministry Approach," 2.

3. Carl E. Larson and Frank M. J. LaFasto, *Teamwork* (Newbury Park: Sage Publications, 1989), 94.

4. Anderson, *Multiple Ministries,* 20–21.

5. Brown, *Church Staff Teams That Win,* 26.

6. Dwight D. Eisenhower, *At Ease* (Garden City, N.J.: Doubleday, 1967), 253.

7. Katzenbach and Smith, *The Wisdom of Teams,* 3.

8. Stephen R. Covey, *The Seven Habits of Highly Effective People* (New York: Simon and Schuster, 1989), 49.

9. Thomas Quick, *Successful Team Building* (New York: AMACOM, 1992), 76.

10. Drucker, *Managing the Non-Profit Organization,* 124.

11. Katzenbach and Smith, *The Wisdom of Teams,* 144.

12. Thomas A. Kayser, *Mining Group Gold* (El Segundo, Calif.: Serif Publishing, 1990), xiii.

13. McDowell, "10 Ways to Support Your Staff," 39.

14. Quick, *Successful Team Building,* 25.

15. George Bullard, *Champions Book Notes* 1, no. 9 (May 1998), 2.

16. Easum, "Teams," 8.

17. Dale E. Galloway, "Building a Winning Staff Team," *Net Results* XX, no. 1 (January 1999): 27–28.

18. Katzenbach and Smith, *The Wisdom of Teams,* 60.

19. Glenn H. Varney, *Building Productive Teams* (San Francisco: Jossey-Bass, 1989), 124.

20. James F. Hind, "The Perfect Executive," *Wall Street Journal,* December 15, 1989.

21. Adapted from Dan Reiland, "Coaching Leaders in Developing Pastoral Staff" (lecture presented at the Church in the 21st Century conference, Dallas, Texas, January 1999).

Resources

Anderson, Martin. *Multiple Ministries*. Minneapolis: Augsburg, 1965.

Brown, Jerry W. *Church Staff Teams That Win*. Nashville: Convention Press, 1979.

Donnelly, Dody. *Team: Theory and Practice of Team Ministry*. New York: Paulist Press, 1977.

Henkelmann, Ervin F., and Stephan J. Carter. *How to Develop a Team Ministry and Make It Work*. St. Louis: Concordia, 1985.

Howse, W. L. *The Church Staff and Its Work*. Nashville: Broadman Press, 1959.

Judy, Marvin T. *The Multiple Staff Ministry*. Nashville: Abingdon Press, 1969.

Larson, Carl E., and Frank M. J. LaFasto. *Teamwork*. Newbury Park: Sage Publications, 1989.

Mitchell, Kenneth R. *Multiple Staff Ministries*. Philadelphia: Westminister Press, 1988.

Nuechterlein, Anne Marie. *Improving Your Multiple Staff Ministry*. Minneapolis: Augsburg, 1989.

Nuechterlein, Anne Marie, and Celia Allison Hahn. *The Male-Female Church Staff.* Washington, D.C.: Alban Institute, 1990.

Parker, Glenn M. *Team Players Handbook.* 1990; reprint, San Francisco: Jossey-Bass, 1990, 1996.

Schaller, Lyle E. *The Multiple Staff and the Larger Church.* Nashville: Abingdon Press, 1980.

———. *The Senior Minister.* Nashville: Abingdon Press, 1988.

Schey, Stephen L., and Walt Kallestad. *Team Ministry: A Workbook for Getting Things Done.* Nashville: Abindgon Press, 1996.

Sweet, Herman J. *The Multiple Staff in the Local Church.* Philadelphia: Westminster Press, 1963.

Wedel, Leonard E. *Building and Maintaining a Church Staff.* Nashville: Broadman, 1966.

Westing, Harold J. *Church Staff Handbook.* Grand Rapids: Kregel, 1997.

Wiebe, Ronald W., and Bruce A. Rowlison. *Let's Talk about Church Staff Relationships.* Alhambra, Calif.: Green Leaf, 1983.

Williams, Pat. *The Magic of Teamwork: Proven Principles for Building a Winning Team.* Nashville: Thomas Nelson, 1997.

Services Available

Dr. Gary L. McIntosh speaks to numerous churches, organizations, schools, and conventions each year. Services available include keynote presentations at major meetings, seminars, and workshops; training courses; and ongoing consultation.

For a live presentation of the material found in *Staff Your Church for Growth* or to request a catalog of materials or other information on Dr. McIntosh's availability and ministry, contact:

The McIntosh Church Growth Network
PO Box 892589
Temecula, CA 92589-2589
909-506-3086

On the World Wide Web at:
www.MCINTOSHCGN.COM
or
www.CHURCHGROWTHNETWORK.COM

Dr. Gary L. McIntosh is a nationally known author, speaker, educator, consultant, and professor of Christian Ministry and Leadership at Talbot School of Theology, Biola University, located in La Mirada, California. He has written extensively in the field of pastoral ministry, leadership, generational studies, and church growth.

Dr. McIntosh received his B.A. from Colorado Christian University in Biblical Studies, an M.Div. from Western C.B. Seminary in Pastoral Studies, and a D.Min. from Fuller Theological Seminary in Church Growth Studies.

As president of the *McIntosh Church Growth Network,* a church consulting firm he founded in 1989, Dr. McIntosh has served over 500 churches in 53 denominations throughout the United States and Canada. The 1995 and 1996 president of the American Society for Church Growth, he edits both the *Church Growth Network* newsletter and the *Journal of the American Society for Church Growth.*